Seattle's Nippon Kan

The discovery of Seattle's other history.
By Edward and Elizabeth Burke

ENCHI YAMASHITA
902-E. ALLISON ST.
SEATTLE

Seattle's Nippon Kan consumed twenty years of our marriage and shaped my life and that of my wife Elizabeth. We fell in love with the Nippon Kan, learning and sharing its' history and culture. This is the story of the hall, how it came to be built, its' early years, its' fall into dereliction and its' glorious renaissance.

This book is dedicated to the memory of Elizabeth Burke who died on Christmas Day, 2010.

Author Biographies

Edward Burke was born in New York City in 1930. His early schooling was in England. He returned to New York in 1946 to earn a degree in fine arts at the University of the City of New York. Following service in the United States Army during the Korean Conflict he earned an additional degree at the College of Architecture of the University of Washington. He managed The Burke Associates, Architects and planners in Seattle for twenty six years. His fellow professionals elected him to the **College of Fellows of the American Institute of Architects**, an honor shared by only five percent of the architects in the United States. In 1969 he purchased the derelict hotel containing the Nippon Kan. He restored the building in 1980. In 1990 the Emperor of Japan bestowed on him the **Order of the Sacred Treasure with Gold Rays and Rosette.**

Elizabeth Burke was born in New York City in 1932. She grew up in the Bronx, graduating from Hunter College Summa Cum Laude. She met Edward, her soul mate, when she was 13 and he 15. They were married for 59 years. After their first daughter Linda was born, the couple moved to Seattle where they were blessed with two more daughters, Sheila Siobhan and Allison Patricia. They raised their children in Rainier Valley. In 1965 Elizabeth entered Seattle Pacific University where she earned a Masters Degree in Creative Education. She taught a class for gifted children at Seattle Country Day School until 1980 when her husband completed renovation of the Kobe Park Building containing the Nippon Kan. She then became manager of the theatre and led historic tours of the International District. Under her guidance the heritage and life of the Nippon Kan were restored.

Edward and Elizabeth shared all of the grief and joy involved in restoring and operating the Nippon Kan. Edward firmly believes that the awards he received for this work were earned by both he and his wife.

Table of Contents

Chapter 1

Why the Nippon Kan was built

The Nippon Kan came into being a mere fifty eight years after the settlement of Seattle. Its construction was a direct product of Seattle's Asian American history during that period.

In 1851 the Denny party sailed into shallow waters at Alki Point and spent a harsh wet winter. The next year they moved across Puget Sound to a much more hospitable area and named it after a local Indian, Chief Sealth, or Seattle. Doc Maynard laid out parcels of land to sell on a small spit of land with mud to the south and east but excellent deep water on the west just south of the area now known as Pioneer Square. My sketch shows Seattle's pioneer industries. Yesler's log mill and dock were at the north end and Madame Damnable's house was at the south end of the village. Seattle's future as a center of industry and entertainment was established. An 1856 map had the words "thronged with Indians" marked on the ridge above the settlement. This was the year of Seattle's Indian War. It only lasted three days but news of the war ruined the real estate market. Seattle grew slowly.

SEATTLE IN 1855
COPYRIGHT 1979 EDWARD AND ELIZABETH BURKE

Seattle Settlement 1855   9

The Chinese Experience

Chin Chun Hock arrived in Seattle only eight years after the Denny's landed and was among the early settlers of Seattle. Chinese immigrants had flocked to the United States following the discovery of gold in California. They worked the mines and with the Irish formed the labor force which built the railroads in the United States. The Chinese were not all laborers. Many were businessmen. Those with English language skills became very successful as labor contractors providing work forces to carve out and tame the wilderness. In 1860 Chin Chun Hock formed the Wa Chong Company located just south of Pioneer Square on 1st Avenue South. Seattle was then little more than a one street town. The street was mud and the sidewalks were made of wood planking. The University of Washington can be seen in the Wa Chong store photo. It was located in the distant woods on a site now occupied by the Four Seasons Hotel. The University still owns five blocks in the heart of downtown Seattle. Not a bad investment!

Wa Chong store

10

First evidence of Seattle Chinese   11

Our first photographic evidence of the Chinese in Seattle is an 1874 picture of the
Hop Sing Laundry located on Mill Street (Now Yesler Way). The store fronted on
Pioneer Square. The Hop Sing Tong was very powerful on the west coast. Its
influence extended into the 1980s.

Yesler had skidded logs down Mill Street. The staid folks lived and attended
churches to the north. The brawlers, loggers and prostitutes lived to the south on a
peninsula of land extending into the mud flats. Ultimately this area acquired the
pejorative name "Skid Row".

In the 1970s, the supposed renewal of Pioneer Square to the way it was in the
"Good old days" was historically incorrect. The old days were the "Bad old days".
Gunslingers and gamblers brawled in the streets. The area was called the
"Tenderloin" because at least five bawdy houses were operating on Washington
Street between First and Fourth Avenues. Considering Seattle had a population of
only 2,000 at the time, the "seamstresses" formed a significant part of the
population. This was the only area the Chinese were allowed to live and have their
businesses in.

In those days brothels were an accepted part of life. Joshua Green, a survivor of Seattle's early days, told me that Lou Graham, one of Seattle's best known brothel managers, sent her girls out in a carriage driving along First Avenue to advertise the business every day. He said she bailed the school system out twice when they couldn't pay the teachers. Joshua had been a member of one of Seattle's two volunteer fire teams. Owners of burning stores gave gifts of merchandise to the first team to arrive at a fire. Joshua said they only had a problem with this system when a fire broke out in Lou Graham's parlor. One member of Joshua's team was upstairs with one of the ladies of the house. When a fire broke out he slid down a drain pipe, pushed in the front door and cried "Team One is here" just as Team Two arrived. Joshua declined to tell me how the issue was resolved.

The Tenderloin District   12

Railroads over the mud flats   13

Fremont, Ballard and Columbia City were all separate logging towns. Huge trees were being felled on Beacon Hill to the south for shipment to San Francisco. Short railways were developed over the mud flats to get the logs to the waterfront. These railways occupied the area now known as the International District. Chin Chun Hock supplied the labor to build these railways.

While Seattle only had a small Chinese community its leaders controlled a substantial number of Chinese working in the hinterland. The Chinese worked in the gold fields of Montana, logging camps and canneries on Puget Sound, hop farms and wherever hard work had to be done. The post civil war railroad construction brought a great influx of Chinese to the northwest. Of the 25,000 men it took to drive the Northern Pacific through the Cascade Mountains 15,000 were Chinese.

Building the railroads through the Cascade Mountains   14A

Chin Gee Hee arrived in Seattle in1870. In 1905 he returned to China as a millionaire. He developed the Sunning Railroad, a major line and the first built by a Chinese businessman. While in Seattle he served as labor contractor for construction of the Walla Walla line. He made money anyway he could just as Denny, Yesler, Doc Maynard and the other pioneers did. He got our railroads built and helped thousands of Chinese fleeing starvation in drought plagued Canton.

Chin Gee Hee   14B

In the 1880s the United States faced major unemployment and the Chinese were blamed. Sound familiar? Following completion of major projects in the hinterlands Chinese laborers crowded the cities engendering hatred by their presence. In 1882 Congress passed the Asian Exclusion Act prohibiting entry of Chinese laborers into the United States and precluding those of Mongolian race from becoming citizens. The Civil War determined that Blacks and Whites could become citizens. It did nothing for the Chinese.

Up and down the west coast, Chinatowns were destroyed and Chinese labor camps were attacked. Labor leaders called for the ouster of the Chinese. In Issaquah, Indians and Whites attacked the Chinese who worked in the hop fields. Three Chinese were killed and the others forced out of town. The men who did this were acquitted.

In Tacoma over 200 Chinese were put on open carts and sent out of town in midwinter. One died of exposure. The next day the remaining Chinese were put on a train and sent to Portland. The Tacoma leaders who accomplished this outrage were so proud of their work they had a group picture taken to commemorate the event.

1. A. U. Mills.
2. M. Kaufman.
3. E. G. Bacon.
4. John Budlong.
5. Jacob Ralph.
6. H. A. Stevens.
13. William Christie.
7. James Wickersham.
8. Chas. Johnson.
9. John Forbes.
14. D. B. Hannah.
10. M. F. Brown.
11. Henry S. Bixler.
12. John A. McGouldric

COMMITTEE OF FIFTEEN,

Having Charge of the Anti-Chinese Agitation in Tacoma. W. T.

15

Judge Burke defends the Chinese in Seattle   16A

In 1886 a mob marched Seattle's Chinese to a boat to ship them out. When the captain declared the boat full there was the possibility that the remaining Chinese would be killed. Judge Burke led the militia to quell the riot. The Sheriff supported the rioters and tried to arrest him. Burke would have been lynched had martial law not been declared. Most Chinese left Seattle. Chin Gee Hee and a few other leaders remained in the city.

So why did the Chinese return? In 1889 Seattle's downtown was destroyed by fire. The undersized wooden water pipes gave out so buildings were dynamited to form a fire break. Most of the downtown was destroyed. Chin Gee Hee and other labor contractors brought Chinese back to rebuild the city.

Seattle destroyed by fire.   16B

Back in business in tents   16C

The merchants were in business the next day operating out of tents. The "seamstresses" did the same the next night. They had different working hours but all wanted to rebuild Seattle as it had been, or almost as it had been.
The city passed an ordinance requiring all buildings be constructed of masonry. They also decided to raise the streets in the Tenderloin area ten feet to improve

drainage and get out of the mud. The property owners rebuilt with two main floors. The lower one was used for the first five years. When the city finished raising the streets, owners bridged across the lower sidewalks to the higher entrance. All of this work required labor. The Wa Chong Company and labor contractors like Chin Gee Hee and Goon Dip provided this labor.

Chin Gee Hee built the first brick building constructed in the Tenderloin after the fire. In the rebuilding process the Hop Sing built a substantial brick structure on S. Washington Street. There was also the Quong Tuck Building. The Canton Building was erected on the corner of 3rd Avenue South. The first Chinatown was established.

Seattle after the fire 1891   17

By 1891 Seattle was substantially rebuilt but there was hardly anyone living on Beacon Hill to the south. To the east the Central Area had only a scattering of houses and to the north of Lake Union they were still logging trees. Discovery of gold in Alaska and the Klondike would change this. Seattle became a major source of supplies for the thousands who steamed to the north. Rather than relying on extractive industries Seattle developed a supply and manufacturing economy. In the next thirteen years the city tripled its population. Imagine that, tripled its population!! Labor was needed to handle this growth but Chinese labor was not welcomed. Japanese immigrants began to fill the need.

Japanese Immigration

For centuries, Japan had been isolated from the world by the edicts of the Tokugawas. In 1853, one year after Seattle was established; Commodore Perry sailed into Tokyo bay with a flotilla of gunships to open Japan to western countries. The Japanese complied but wisely decided that to survive as a nation they too needed gunships. Twenty five years later, in 1878, the Japanese navy steamed into Puget Sound and visited Seattle.

The Japanese had made a radical change in their way of life. The samurai class had been defeated using western military equipment and the Emperor Meiji had ushered in an era of westernization. The Japanese chose to model their government on that of England, their military on that of Germany and their economy on that of the United States. There was even discussion of adopting English as the national language. These radical societal changes caused many Japanese to immigrate.

The first Japanese settlers arrived in Seattle in 1879 just a few years before the Anti Chinese riots. We could find no references to how the Japanese fared during the riots although it is unlikely that they went to the expense of creating "I am Japanese" buttons. From the start they were viewed as distinct from the Chinese.

The United States wanted trade with Japan. Japan was not competing with the United States so our government chose not to apply the Asian Exclusion Act to the Japanese. Japanese were deemed not to be of the Mongolian race.

The rate of immigration increased further following Japan's 1904 war with Russia. The Japanese were ecstatic when the Russian navy was defeated near Vladivostok. They had defeated a European power. Unfortunately Japan then experienced a deep recession. Unemployment and unrest among social activists led men with new ideas to come to the United States. They took jobs in mining, logging, farming and commerce at first working for Chinese labor contractors then later for Japanese contractors. As was the case with the Chinese, not all of the Japanese immigrants were laborers. Many were well educated and started businesses in Seattle. A good number of them became involved with Seattle real estate and managed hotels in the International District.

Restaurant   19A

Produce company   19B

Logging camp   19C

Inside Furuya's bank   19D

Company picnic at Furuya house on Bainbridge Island   19E

Two Japanese banks were established in Seattle, the Furuya Bank and the
Sumitomo bank.   They were founded by savvy businessmen who realized the
potential which the influx of Japanese immigrants provided. The Furuya Bank was
located in the area southeast of Pioneer Square. The Japanese immigrants settled to
the east of the bank forming a distinct Japan Town (Nihon Machi) adjacent to the
Chinese settlement and the Union Station.

A Major Upheaval of Chinatown and the Nihon Machi

R. H. Thompson, City Engineer was a visionary who shaped the future of Seattle. He established the Cedar River Watershed and built a six foot diameter wood pipe to bring water to the city. He established City Light and the Port Authority. He located Seattle's sewer outfall. He had large areas of the city regraded.

Three of his projects disrupted Chinatown and the Nihon Machi. He struck an agreement in 1904 with the Great Northern Railway Company to build the King Street Station on S. Jackson Street and 5th Avenue S. Their main line to the north would run through a tunnel under 4th Avenue. He regraded the area between Yesler Way and Beacon Hill. To add insult to injury Thompson rerouted 2nd Avenue South through the heart of the Chinese and Japanese areas.

Regrading projects   20

At the southern end of the downtown there was a trolley line that climbed Washington Street on its way to Renton. When it reached 6th Avenue South, the passengers had to get out and push it to the top of the hill, then get on quickly because it rapidly took off down the other side. R. H. Thompson decided to cut a major path through that hill in 1908. The dirt from the excavation was used to fill the mud flats. S. Jackson Street was lowered eighty feet. Imagine the relocation of people and the environmental impact statement that would be required today.

The graders operated like giant gophers. First they developed the streets, then they removed the dirt piles between. Small buildings were moved. Larger buildings were propped up and gradually lowered. The Japanese Baptist Church on Jackson Street had to be lowered thirty feet. The regraders borrowed a technique used in the Alaska gold fields and had an easy way to get the dirt from the top of the hills to the bottom. They used high pressure hoses, turned the earth into mud and it went downhill all by itself. Dirt from the railway tunnel was tracked out to S. Washington St. then sluiced to the south from there. For several years the entire area was a giant mud hole.

MOVING MOUNTAINS

HOSING THE HILLSIDES 2

2nd Avenue rerouted   21A

Sluicing the hills down   21B

But when they were through, land for the railway yards and industrial expansion had been created right next to downtown and right next to one of the best ports in the world. Seattle's future was assured. The first land created was called the

International District and in those days it really was international. Hotels sprang up to house the large influx of single male immigrants who flocked to Seattle from all over the world. There was a little Italy to the south and a Japan Town to the north. A new Chinatown was established in the middle.

Redeveloped land   22

Relocating Chinatown

Chinatown had been severely impacted by the massive projects undertaken by the city and was ready for change. Goon Dip, a prominent member of the Chinese community had become wealthy. He had been designated honorary Chinese Consul for the 1904 Alaska Yukon Pacific Exposition held in Seattle and had helped finance construction of a large Chinese Pavilion at the Fairgrounds. Seattle was booming and land was available. He was one of those who persuaded the Chinese to move to the area east of the King Street Station. In 1910, he himself built the Milwaukee Hotel on S. King Street at the center of the three and a half block area which his community acquired and called Chinatown. As my good friend Ben Woo once said "There are no Chinatowns in China, they only exist in the United States".

Goon Dip Young building on S. King Street   23A

The Hop Sing, Bing Kung, Hip Sing and Suey Sing organizations all built their own major buildings and created a new Chinatown. The street levels were occupied by stores. Small hotel rooms were above the stores and at the top were the association halls with balconies in the style of Southern China.

Bing Kung Tong   23B

Association Ceremonial Room   23C

The Asian Exclusion Act of 1882 stopped the immigration of Chinese before male immigrants could bring brides from China. In 1900 there were 33 Chinese men in Seattle for every woman. Interracial marriage was illegal. The combination was genocidal and socially debilitating. Chinatown was primarily a community of men and developed all the vices which such a community can create. While the Exclusion law could be circumvented it was difficult. Goon Dip was able to bring a wife from China but this was impossible for most of the Chinese. Accordingly Chinatown did not grow. It also became an area with a high crime rate.

Other developers invested in the regraded area. One of these was a millionaire who made his fortune in the Yukon. He at one time owned four city blocks in the regraded area and developed hotels which he placed in the hands of Japanese managers. He married the madam of a bawdy house and invited Seattle's society to a reception at his house on Queen Anne Hill. When they did not show up he went down to Pioneer Square and found many guests eager to attend. By a strange coincidence his home later became the official residence of the Consul General of Japan in Seattle.

Nihon Machi

At the time of the regrading many buildings in the Japanese settlement were destroyed. When the new land was created to the south of Jackson Street the Japanese immigrants expanded into this area and managed most of the buildings surrounding Chinatown. Unlike the Chinese community, the Japanese community was slated for major growth. Japanese were able to immigrate freely and bring picture brides from Japan. By 1924 the Japanese community was balanced and growing. In 1917 there were 21 midwives working in the Japanese American community. All were kept very busy. Japanese Americans even established a three story hospital on King Street east of Chinatown. Japanese Americans were being born and were a major part of Seattle's growth.

When the area surrounding Chinatown became too small to accommodate the community and as the need for family rather than hotel housing grew, the community expanded up the hill to Yesler Way and east to 16th Avenue creating an enormous Nihon Machi. In terms of size, the Nihon Machi was fifteen times that of Chinatown and engulfed it. The commercial heart of the Nihon Machi was at S. Main Street and 6th Avenue South but Japanese American businesses extended throughout the International District.

Calvin Schmid's pioneering social analysis mapped this growth. While restrictive real estate practices played a major factor in the concentration of the Japanese American community and restricted its nibbling advancement into adjacent housing there were several other factors at play. Immigrants tended to cluster in communities containing services designed to serve them. Religious and social organizations promoted proximity of similar ethnic interests. Ballard's concentration of Scandinavian immigrants was a case in point. In the Japanese American community common language was a major factor. The Japanese language has an entirely different structure from European languages. While other immigrants could quickly master English, this was not the case with Japanese immigrants. It was more comfortable to be clustered in the Nihon Machi where the language and customs could be maintained. Even smells tend to keep people in touch with similar people. The Italian community spread to the south east down Rainier Valley to the point that it became known pejoratively as Garlic Gulch. Consumption of garlic changed not only the breath of the Italian immigrants; it changed the odor of the sweat their bodies exuded. Non Italians found this offensive and preferred to live in other areas. The Japanese immigrants ate fish and miso soup giving their bodies an entirely different odor from that of European meat eating immigrants. This was yet another factor making the Nihon Machi a very comfortable place for Japanese Americans to live in. It became a ghetto due to both external forces and internal wishes.

As a young professional I lived in Southeast Seattle near three Synagogues. Knowing I was active in the civil rights movement and opposed to any form of ghetto a Jewish friend introduced me to his Rabbi. The Rabbi was concerned that his neighborhood was changing and "different" people were moving into it. He wanted my opinion of his plan to have his congregation buy any house that became vacant and save it to sell only to Jewish people, preferably those who adhered to his sect. I was appalled. He was contemplating the establishment of a self imposed ghetto. While I sympathized with his desire to cluster his flock around him I pointed out the unfortunate results ghetto living patterns had produced in Nazi Germany and many other countries.

Unfortunately for the Japanese American immigrants, the Nihon Machi became a distinct ghetto. It housed the largest minority in Seattle. It became an easy target for discrimination and prejudice.

A map based on information contained in "Issei" written by Kazuo Ito shows the extent of Japanese businesses in the core of the International District.

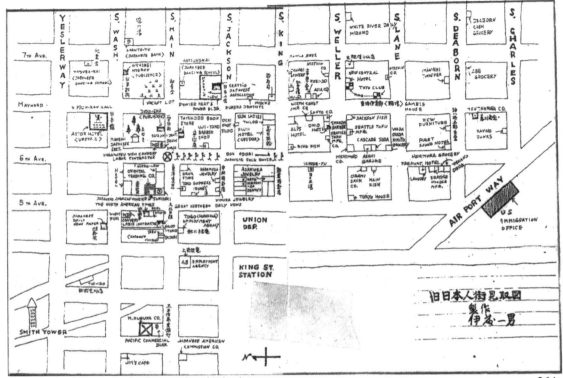

Japanese businesses in the International District   26A

S. Main Street, commercial heart of the Nihon Machi.   26B

The Japanese were not allowed in Seattle theatres unless they sat in the balcony. They were a proud people and decided to build their own theatre, the Nippon Kan.

The Nippon Kan was needed not just for entertainment. As the community grew there was a need for a meeting space which would accommodate many people. A community meeting held in 1905 illustrates this need with a large segment of the community crowded into a basement space. Only six women are shown in this photograph as the early community was primarily male.

1905 Crowded community meeting   27

The Astor Hotel

One of the hotels built in the Nihon Machi to house the influx of Japanese immigrants was the Astor Hotel containing the Nippon Kan.

The upper two floors were built with small single room units. These units shared toilets down the hall. The lack of bathing facilities fit into the cultural background of men who had enjoyed going to commercial bath houses in Japan. Many bath houses flourished in the Japanese American community. One of them was located in the Panama Hotel only two blocks away.

The main floor of the Astor Hotel housed the Nippon Kan. Stores were located on the street level below although the steepness of S. Washington Street and the bustle of the commercial heart of the community two blocks away limited their viability. One of the storefronts became a dressing area for theatre events. It was connected to the Nippon Kan by a narrow interior stairway at the rear of the hall. Two of the storefronts were used as the Yorita print shop. (Ben, one of the Yorita children was actually born in the Astor Hotel). The westerly bay was used for music lessons. A store front located at the southeast corner of the building was on the same level as the Nippon Kan and catered to the needs of theatre users renting seat cushions and selling frozen bananas.

Yorita print shop   28

History of the Building's Ownership

The Astor Hotel was designed by Thompson and Thompson Architects, a father and son firm. It was built in 1909 by the Cascade Investment Company. This company had been formed by Takahashi, Hirade and Tsukuno using a token Caucasian to complete the transaction. A prominent banker, Masajiro Furuya later acquired the structure and sold stock to raise capital.

Nippon Kan Stock Certificate   29A

By 1910 the community had developed a representative structure known as the
Japanese Association. The photo below shows an advertising screen hanging
behind members of this group posing on the stage of the Nippon Kan. The screen
was an asbestos screen used to protect the audience should a fire break out on stage
but it also served as a means for local stores to advertize their businesses. The
screen was the first screen used in the Nippon Kan and is now preserved at the
Wing Luke Asian Museum in Seattle.

1915 Japanese Association meeting   29B

In 1924 a terrible earthquake in Japan bankrupted many of the banks in that country and the economic impact was felt in Seattle. Of possibly greater impact was the passage by the US Congress in 1924 of legislation which extended to the Japanese all of the injustices of the Asian Exclusion Act. This terminated the annual influx of Japanese immigrants on which the banks had relied for their growth. Both the Sumitomo and Furuya banks were affected. This was followed in the early 30s by the great U.S. depression. When the Furuya bank was bankrupted, the Astor Hotel reverted to creditors. The Tanaka family operated the hotel until the Evacuation. When the Tanakas were interned a Caucasian acquaintance, Frank Hocking, who had operated an ice cream parlor south of Jackson took over. A lack of income from the Nippon Kan and rent restrictions on the upstairs apartments made the property a losing proposition and it reverted to the Continental Land Bank Company.

In 1946, following the end of World War II, Seiji Nakamura bought the property. He and his family lived in and managed the apartments upstairs. His daughter had danced in the hall prior to the Evacuation and is the dancer located to the right in the painting on this book's cover. His hope was to restore the Nippon Kan but community interest was non-existent and the project too large to tackle. Seiji Nakamura sold the property in May 1967 to Abie Label, operator of single room occupancy hotels.

Following a fatal fire in the Ozark Hotel, a single room occupancy hotel, a City Ordinance was passed requiring fire sprinkler systems in similar hotels. The cost of installation could not be recovered in the rents which occupants could afford. Most of these hotels closed. While this ensured that there would not be any loss of life due to fires, it resulted in a massive loss of housing for those who could least afford it and who were forced to become street people. The City of Seattle is still struggling at high cost to solve a problem that, with the best of intentions, was caused by the city itself. The Astor Hotel sat vacant until we purchased it in 1969.

Chapter 2
The Nippon Kan's Early Years

From 1909 until January 1942, the Nippon Kan served as a focal point for the Japanese American community. In the early days the mostly male immigrants, Issei (first generation), shaped the activities in the hall. Political debates took place between the Red and White parties. Ibsen's play "A Doll's House" was performed with an all male cast. As picture brides immigrated, traditional dance and music societies performed on the stage. Their American children, Nisei, (second generation) engaged in activities common to other American children. They joined the Boy Scouts, had dance clubs with flapper dancers, baseball and University Student Associations. Issei brought the culture of Japan to the Nippon Kan. Nisei absorbed this and enriched it with their American experience. At the beginning, when a political forum was held, a male audience packed the Nippon Kan. There was a sense of freedom which attracted political activists to Seattle. The community had several Japanese language newspapers. Two magazines were published. Followers of the leftist leader Sen Katayama flocked to Seattle and Meiji bohemians orated late into the night on the cause of the rights of man. Later many became statesmen, ministers and attorneys. The theme of one speaker epitomized their hard working ethic: "Self Reliance and 'Perspirationism'. A typical program from 1910 had ambitious content for an evening of listening:

Debate Program

Concerning the Election of the President of the
Japanese Association in Washington State.................................Nanzan Yokoyama
My Opinion on Current Events..Tengai Morioka
About the Election of the Vice President of the
Japanese Association in Washington State............................Keinojo Sugiyama
The Public and I..Goro Taketa
(Title not Decided)..Yozan Nishizawa
Japanese Association Past and Future...................................Musen Shinomiya
Senzo Hiranuma and the House of Peers..............................Seiran Takeuchi
(Title not Decided)..Katsunari Sasaki
(Title not Decided)..Shigetaka Yokoya
Destruction or Unity? ....Yasuzo Suzuki
(Title not Decided) ....Bokukin Uno
Moderator ....Shiro Fujioka

The Hall saw many visiting evangelists. Churches played an important role in the early immigrant community. Many of the immigrants learned of American ways from missionaries and took language classes even before they left Japan. Once in a strange country they found assistance and companionship in local congregations. The Catholic Mary knoll organization, Baptist , Methodist Episcopal churches, the Seattle Buddhist Temple, and many others acted in this capacity. Early community churches had limited facilities and used the Nippon Kan when they needed more space. Because the Nippon Kan did not contain a piano, when one was required, it was hauled from the Baptist Church located on S. Jackson Street up the hill to the Nippon Kan. This was not an easy task.

1916 Kanemori Tsurin, Japanese evangelist   32A   1915 Memorial service for Shig Osawa's sister   32B

When we purchased the Nippon Kan, Shig Osawa was the oldest living Nisei in the community. He was sitting in the front row of the photo showing a community meeting prior to the construction of the Nippon Kan. The photo of his sister's memorial service in the Nippon Kan indicates yet another religious use to which the hall was put. Notice the very stern Caucasian lady dressed in black sitting in the front row. Presumably she represented one of the many church organizations which helped the early immigrants. Her attire is in great contrast to the clothing of the family member sitting on the far left of the front row.

As church congregations grew and were able to build larger facilities the need for and the use of the Nippon Kan for their events diminished although use of the hall for fundraisers continued and grew.

1911 Ohashi, extreme left rear row   33A   Mr. Ohashi as a samurai   33B

The story of the Nippon Kan is one of people and their use of the hall both before and after the Evacuation. The 1911 photo of a young Ohashi graduating from the Anacortes Elementary School stands in sharp contrast to his later photo posing as a samurai performing in the Nippon Kan. Mr. Ohashi was a frequent performer in the Nippon Kan before the Evacuation. He was the first of three generations to be involved with the hall.

Following the restoration of the theatre Ohashi's daughter Fumi Higashi performed in the first play produced in the Nippon Kan. She used her maiden name "Ohashi" to honor her father and became a regular performer with the Northwest Asian American Theatre group. Mr. Ohashi's grandson Mike Higashi was a dentist and became one of the first commercial tenants to take space in the building following its renovation. Three generations were associated with the building housing the Nippon Kan.

1913 Toyo Club members   34A

The Toyo Club sitting precariously outside the main entrance on Maynard Avenue illustrates the extreme slope on which the Nippon Kan was built. When handicapped accessibility laws were passed in the 1980s we found it was impossible to comply with the law's requirements although we were able to accommodate wheelchairs by bringing residents of the Keiro Nursing home and others through the stage door.

1920 Japanese Sewing Club just east of the Nippon Kan   34B

This photo of the sewing club shows how the steep slope continued to the north. The community was very tightly knit and had a host of clubs and organizations bringing the Japanese immigrants together. Hosoe Kodama is third from the left in the front row. Her story is relayed later in this book.

For Sumo wrestling, four large poles were set up on the stage of the Nippon Kan. Many Nisei who visited the hall during our tenure remembered coming to the Judo competitions from Auburn, Tacoma, Bainbridge Island and other surrounding communities. One of them, James Matsuoka, never forgot one such event. A Sensei (master teacher) was visiting from Japan and demonstrating holds with young practitioners on the stage. When Jim tackled him the Sensei slipped and Jim was awarded a point. Jim said that it was a big mistake on his part for the Sensei then proceeded to demonstrate to the audience how to handle a beginner. Jim said that he was bounced on every square foot of the stage and learned his lesson the hard way.

Rival groups were always springing up enhancing the competition. The opening ceremony of the Seattle branch of Dai Nippon Butokukai (martial arts club) took place on the Nippon Kan stage in 1937.

1941 Sumo wrestling team   35

But traditional Japanese sports were not the only activity for young Japanese Americans. The Taiyo Baseball club gained acclaim in regional competitions and held many fund raising events in the Nippon Kan.

Taiyo Baseball Team   36A

1937 Fund Raiser for Taiyo baseball Team   36B

The culture contrast of the team in baseball gear versus the amateur performance they gave on the Nippon Kan stage is amazing. The production was directed by Osho san Nakamura, one of several esteemed producers of Nippon Kan events.

Stories of Japan, Kabuki , Noh and Kyogen were sources for Nippon Kan productions. Japanese organizations watched events of other groups and tried to excel them. Productions became very elaborate. In May, 1921 the Asahi Club presented "Yuki no Ichira" with authentic costumes matched by a lovely parasol.

1921 Yuki no Ichira   37A

1926 Osho san Arai   37B

The Arai's were among the earliest and most esteemed immigrants. They were leaders in the community and performed on the stage. Family descendants entered the field of architecture and had exemplary careers. Costuming was elaborate judging from the collage of actors shown below.

Montage of performers   37C

Student dancers   37D

1930s Samurai play "Osome hisamatsu"   38A

Samurai play showing hanamichi in place.   38B

In the 1930s Sensei Nakatani produced the samurai play "Osome hisamatsu" written in the 1700s by Chikamatsu. The set contains a house veranda with a garden gate on stage right leading to the hanamichi, a raised walkway which performers used to approach the stage from the rear of the hall. Raucous comments were frequent as actors traversed the rickety hanamichi. A stage prompter was traditionally located on stage right and the theatre had a window on that side of the proscenium so that stage managers could anticipate actors approaching the stage.

Musicians and chanters were traditionally located on stage left. By the 1930s children were an important part of the audience crowding the edge of the stage to catch the action.

1923 Hatsune dance school. Sensei Nakatani dancing with her daughter   39A

The name Hatsune Kai was boldly painted on the stage wall of the Nippon Kan. This was Madame Nakatani's dance group. Madame Nakatani trained many fine classical dancers some of whom returned to the hall following its renovation in 1980. She was a major force in retaining the cultural arts traditions brought from Japan. The sets for her productions were extremely elaborate and must have taken enormous effort to get into place and remove before the next show.

Biwa Society   39B

But traditional theatrical arts performed by amateurs and Hollywood actors such as Sesshu Hayakawa and Sojin Kamiyama were not all that filled the stage. There were many music groups among which the Shumi-no-kai was very active promoting operatic voice recitals. Many well known musicians performed on the stage. Tamaki Miura, Toshiko Sekiya and Yoshie Fujiwara, singers from Japan, all performed at the Nippon Kan. Tamaki Miura was a friend of Giacomo Puccini, influenced his work and sang the role of Madama Butterfly at the New York Metropolitan Opera Company. In 1925 she performed a series of operatic arias in the Nippon Kan. In the same era Sugi Machi performed in the hall and throughout the west coast and Europe. She was hailed as the Seattle Japanese Nightingale. She premiered a Japanese opera "Sakura" in the Hollywood Bowl. The event was such a success it was given an unprecedented second showing.

1925 Tamaki Miura with of the Seattle Japanese Girls Club   40 A

Program for Tamaki Miura's visit   40B

Seattle's Nippon Kan also launched many musical careers. Miyoshi Sugimachi, Miyo Kajiwara (violinists) and Tomi Kanazawa who sang Madame Butterfly in Europe made their start in Seattle. Shisui Miyashita, composer, conductor and musician organized a club with over 40 music lovers.

1936 Shisui Miyashita with the Seattle Symphony Orchestra featuring pianist Sachiko Ochi,   41

In 1936 Mr. Miyashita conducted his own works with members of the Seattle Symphony and a choir. Mr. Miyashita held concerts three times per year in the hall with admission costs ranging from 50 cents to a dollar. When the Nippon Kan was renovated we enlarged this photo along with several others illustrative of the variety of events which had previously taken place in the hall. We mounted them in the lobby over the entrance to the hall.

It is hard to imagine the energy and vitality which abounded in the community. There were four theatrical groups, four dance groups, koto, shakuhachi, biwa and shamisen groups. The Gyojutsu Kyokai featured Kabuki performances. They held their rehearsals in the Nippon Kan, rested for two days, then played Saturday and Sunday shows with performances averaging twice a month. Scheduling must have been an enormous challenge.

All performances in the Nippon Kan had to be approved by the Toyo Club (a west coast social club with ties to gambling and cannery worker contracting). The Toyo boss (Kin Pachi) controlled all the entertainers. He threw his weight around and carried a gun. It was not a smart move to bypass getting show approval. One performer tried and had his show stopped in the middle when the boss came in, strode up to the stage and said "The show is over". According to Tak Kubota who was present at the time, no one questioned the boss' authority and everyone left the hall. Tak remembered renting out cushions in the hall because the folding seats were very hard after six hours of sitting. The shows were very long and many mothers brought their children to the hall at noon to be sure of a good seat for the night's entertainment. The kabuki tradition of bringing box lunches was practiced in the hall. Events were very social occasions with children running up and down the balcony stairs.

One of Sensei Nakatani's fellow performers deserves special mention. He typified the cross cultural demands experienced by the immigrants.

Kimura enjoying the wild west   42A

Kimura on stage   42B

1929 Shamisen recital, Mr. Kimura chanter   43A.

In love with his new country he had a deep appreciation of his Japanese heritage. Unfortunately he was working in the office of the Consul General in Seattle when Japan attacked Pearl Harbor. He was the first Japanese American arrested in Seattle following the attack on Pearl Harbor.

Associations of musicians performed traditional music of Japan. Schools of biwa, koto, shamisen and shakuhachi players were very active in the hall but as time passed more American activities took place.

1940 Lotus Club Girls Choir   43B

Seattle Japanese Girls Club International Costume Show, ca. 1925   44A

Japanese American flappers.   44B

What the Issei thought of this transition can only be imagined but for the young Japanese Americans it was part of their existence in American culture.

1929 Japanese Girls Club members in an Americanized version of Momotaro   45

Dr. Minoru Masuda, professor at the University of Washington recalled the Shibai, amateur shows which were an eclectic mixture of kabuki, Japanese folk songs, classical dance, kendo, western band music and jazz singing.

Over the years Boy Scout groups used the Nippon Kan and marked their names on the walls of the stage. Members of the Beppu family were noticeable as the Beppu family named their boys after American presidents.

Boy Scouts of America   46A

1940 JACL   46B

The Japanese American Citizens League was formed in Seattle. However, this happy tale of assimilation into the American dream did not reflect reality. International events and the unfortunate tribalism of our species impacted the future of the community and of the Nippon Kan

Chapter 3
National Attitudes Change

While Japan had been viewed favorably when it was a fledgling newcomer on the world scene, its subsequent growth in power was not welcome. The industrial capacity of Japan was displayed in their large pavilion at Seattle's Alaska Yukon Exposition. Japan's military prowess was proven in its successful war with Russia. This was followed by expansion into Mongolia and China directly affected American interests. Japan was becoming extremely competitive in international trade. The United States no longer had a national interest in curbing prejudice.

47

In the 1920s a resurgence of racism hit the west coast. Ku Klux Klan membership in the northwest grew at an alarming rate. When Blacks or Asians were not available, as was the case in Tillamook, Oregon, crosses were burned on the lawns of Catholics. Japanese Americans had been successful, were envied and became a target of racism. Pressure was placed on Congress and in 1924 the Asian Exclusion Act was applied to Japanese immigrants. They could no longer become citizens. California, Oregon and Washington passed laws prohibiting land ownership by persons ineligible for citizenship. Some Issei turned their property over to their children or to white friends. Many lost their land. Many returned to Japan. Even so the community grew because of new born Japanese Americans who were citizens by birth.

Urban Removal

In 1941, Seattle's Nihon Machi was deteriorating. Prostitutes had moved into the area, but that was not the only reason it was selected as the first site for public housing. Twelve city blocks of Japanese ownership were eliminated in the city's second major urban "removal" project. The Japanese Americans stoically moved further east. They completed a new Buddhist Temple east of 12th Avenue in 1941.

Deteriorated hillside housing.   48A

Project   48B   Yesler Terrace Housing

But this relocation was a small problem compared with what was to come.

U.S. at war   49A

When Japan attacked Pearl Harbor, a wave of hysteria hit the United States. Pearl Harbor was a blow to the United States but was a catastrophe for Japanese Americans. Hostility intensified and in February of 1942 the President issued an Executive Order forcing the Evacuation of all persons of Japanese descent to concentration camps located far from Seattle. Two thirds of those incarcerated were American citizens by birth and had been taught in United States schools. Their assimilation was aborted.

Posting notice of the Evacuation order.   49B

The community was given two weeks' notice, could only take with them what they could carry and lost most of their family treasures. They boarded up their homes and businesses. The Nihon Machi and the Nippon Kan became empty shells. Families could not pay their taxes, make mortgage payments or operate their businesses from prison camps. They were temporarily housed in stables at the Puyallup Fairground, sadly misnamed "Camp Harmony". From there most Seattleites were shipped to Minidoka, Idaho. "Shikata ga nai", it can't be helped was their frequent expression of resignation.

While their economic losses were great and their living conditions intolerable, the greatest blows were the social scars which they endured for years following this sad event. The experience of one Japanese American student at Franklin High School epitomized the plight of these young Americans. He was named student of the year in 1941. By December he was suspect and in February 1942 was presumed a traitor and locked in what can only be described as a concentration camp. His sense of betrayal cannot be imagined.

Minidoka

Patriotism in Adversity

In spite of this treatment, thousands of Japanese Americans volunteered from the camps to serve in the United States Army and to offer their lives for a country which had rejected them. Many served in Europe in the 442nd Combat Team, the most highly decorated unit in WWII. Others served in the Pacific, assuming the most dangerous missions. When they returned to Seattle the Nihon Machi was decimated. The Nippon Kan was a derelict shell. Only a few scattered remnants were left to return to.

Truman salutes 442nd Combat Team.   51A

A mother's loss.   51B

Unfortunately racism persisted. War memorials were desecrated to remove the names of Japanese Americans who had died for their country. Japanese American veterans were shunned and insulted. Their parents were not permitted to apply for citizenship until the 1950s. The Alien Land Laws of Washington State were not changed until 1966. It took three attempts at the polls to revise this law.

Given the cultural trauma of these events there were strong divisions within the Japanese American community and there was little desire to publicly celebrate Japanese heritage. Many in the community wished to remain invisible. The churches and Buddhist Temple focused internally. There was no incentive to restore activities in the Nippon Kan so it remained to decay and serve as a pigeon roost for thirty eight years.

Relationship to the Chinese Community

The Chinese and Japanese American communities, while adjacent, had mutual antipathy long before and after WWII.

Chinese attitudes were shaped by the fact that Japan had occupied most of China, committed atrocities on the Chinese population and had taken over many properties in China owned by relatives of Seattle's Chinese. This was not abstract. It was direct human and economic cost to those in Seattle's Chinatown. Because the Asian Exclusion Act was enforced only on Chinese prior to 1924, the Japanese community contained families with children whereas the Chinese community was mostly male. Family Association buildings on King Street were "Family" buildings only in name. There were very few Chinese women and therefore very few families in the Chinese American community. The growth of Chinatown was stagnant whereas by WWII the Nihon Machi was over fifteen times the size of Chinatown. In 1940 the Japanese population numbered 6975 and the Chinese population numbered 1781. These factors caused deep resentment.

In contrast, Japanese attitudes were shaped by their relative success locally and internationally. Bushido and the samurai spirit prevailed in Asia. The Japanese had an empire just like the European countries. They viewed the Chinese as inferior. This was reinforced by the unfortunate results of a largely male Chinese community. In the 1920s and 30s the three and a half block area which comprised Chinatown proper had the highest crime rate in the City of Seattle. Unless engaged in illicit activity the Japanese American community stayed clear of Chinese Americans. They even developed their own Chinese restaurant on the southeast corner of S. Main Street and 6th Avenue South, because they chose not to frequent restaurants operated by Chinese.

One landmark social analysis determined that in the 1930's given a choice, Japanese Americans would prefer to marry a Black than a Chinese American spouse, an amazing statistic given the attitudes of that era.

When the Japanese Americans were evacuated most of Chinese Americans rejoiced and bought "I am Chinese" buttons to differentiate themselves from Japanese Americans. Even today, older Japanese Americans have not forgotten this although their children are fortunately unaware of this history. I was totally oblivious of this complex environment when I became involved in the community.

Chapter 4
Unlikely Restorers

In 1971 when I was President of the Seattle Chapter of the American Institute of Architects, the Chapter considered and wisely decided against purchasing the Astor Hotel for its own use. My partner Leon Bridges and I had formed the first architecture firm in the northwest having a black and a white principal. We were committed to inner city redevelopment. We wanted to show this by moving our office into a building within the Model City area and by investing our own funds in its development. I persuaded Leon that the Astor Hotel should be our project. In retrospect and given our limited resources it was a foolhardy action. We borrowed the down payment and after a short negotiation with the owner, acquired the 28,000 square foot derelict shell. The roof leaked, the windows were broken, fires had been lit by transient squatters and although we were within walking distance of City Hall we were on a dirt street surrounded by blackberry bushes. I took my family to see the building. As we stood in the Nippon Kan with its peeling plaster and pigeons roosting in the balcony all but one of them groaned in dismay. My daughter Sheila clapped her hands exclaiming "Oh Daddy, you bought me my own stage". It would be ten years before she had her first performance on that stage.

Twenty nine years of abandonment   53

Astor Hotel 1971   54A

We could not afford the cost of repairs to prevent water from penetrating through the roof, hotel rooms and light wells. Our office was to be located in three store front bays at street level below the Nippon Kan and had to be kept dry so we hung plastic sheets from the ceiling of the Nippon Kan, placed garbage cans strategically to catch the rainwater and moved our office into the building. This technique worked but required visits to the building on rainy weekends to empty the garbage cans. There are lots of rainy weekends in Seattle. At the time we thought this would be a temporary arrangement. I had doomed myself to nine years of emptying rainwater out of garbage cans.

Rain soaked floors   54B

Uncovered light wells   54C

Future office space for Bridges/Burke Architects
55

Our architectural practice was thriving. We looked forward to a growing economy. Our plan was to develop the whole building including the Nippon Kan into office space. The Nippon Kan was saved by an abrupt change in the economy that brought us close to bankruptcy. We had two false starts with potential government tenants followed by the Boeing economic crash, my partner's departure with his family to Baltimore and disagreements with him regarding the building. We dismantled the partnership. I agreed that he would take the office and accounts we had in Baltimore. I would take the Seattle office including our contract obligations on the building. My wife Betty and I faced hard times.

Repeated delays in our efforts to redevelop the building gave us time to reconsider our plans for the Nippon Kan. My wife and I met with and made friends with Japanese Americans who had been involved in the theatre in the old days. They told us their experiences and shared their photos with us. Our research into Asian American history gave us insights into the severe impact the Evacuation had on their once vibrant community. We came to realize the important role the Nippon Kan had played in the community and committed ourselves to restore the hall to its former glory.

Stage Wall Graffiti

Initially, the writing on the stage walls was our only clue that the theatre had been used by Japanese immigrants. Japanese names were scrawled over all the stage walls.

One of the names was that of John Okada who wrote "No No Boy". This very controversial book described the life after WWII of a Seattle Japanese American who had refused to answer positively two key questions required on the loyalty oath that evacuees were required to sign in the concentration camps. Most Japanese Americans wanted to sweep the Evacuation under the rug and definitely did not want it known that some had renounced their citizenship as a protest for the unconstitutional treatment they had received. We learned that there were many conflicts within and between Japanese American groups. We later understood that these conflicts were a factor in the reticence of Japanese Americans to embrace our plans for the Nippon Kan.

Dianne Anderson showing names   56

56

Discovering the Stage Screen

We had owned the Astor Hotel containing the Nippon Kan four years before we discovered the Nippon Kan's original advertising screen. There was a rack on the rear wall of the stage to hold scrims and scenery drop cloths. It contained a dingy roll of burlap mounted on the uppermost rack. When relatives visited from Florida they helped lower the roll to the stage floor. What a discovery!!! The screen was painted with one meter square advertisements for local stores. We hung it on the rack so it could be viewed.

It was in poor condition so I invited a friend, Henry Trubner, Assistant Director of the Seattle Art museum to evaluate it. His advice was to roll it up and save it for future generations. We couldn't do that. We wanted to share it with others so we left it hanging on the rack. Some advertisements had been painted over. We assumed they belonged to businesses that had not paid for their advertisement.

Author showing visitors the screen

Some advertisers were still in business. Higo's Variety store was still located on the northeastern corner of S. Jackson Street and 6th Avenue South. Higo's advertisement showed a frog, a symbol of thrift in Japan. Previous ads by Higo showed through the fading paint. Before we bought the Astor Hotel I had purchased a lacquered pagoda shaped jewelry box for my wife at Higo's, little knowing that one day I would encounter the store's advertising in a building we owned. Each time Betty opened the music box it played "Sakura". My daughter Allison still treasures it. When the Higo family was evacuated, the family left the boarded up premises in the hands of a Caucasian who protected their building until their return. In gratitude they froze his rent for the rest of his life.

The Nakamura Jewelers ad showed an old Victrola with a dog listening to "His master's voice". The young Nakamura still operated a clock repair store to the east of Higo's on S. Jackson Street. He remembered helping his dad operate the projector and sound system when they showed Japanese movies in the Nippon Kan before the Evacuation.

The Maneki Restaurant ad showed a cat with paw extended. The restaurant had originally been located nearby at 6th Avenue South and S. Washington Street. The restaurant served 'after performance' meals to Nippon Kan performers. It is now located one block to the south. The restaurant continued this tradition following our renovation of the building.

The ad for the milliner's store was unique in showing the type of hat worn by women in the community at the time the screen was in use.

Stage screen advertisement   58

Collecting Artifacts

Friends in the broader community became aware of our peculiar interests and broadened our role in preserving Japanese American history.

Japanese Language School Materials

In the early 1970s, Ken Lothian, Superintendent of Seattle's Water Department called and told me twelve crates of old Japanese books and artifacts were to be auctioned off at a warehouse on Harbor Island. I hurried down to see them. One of the items held by the auction company was an engraved silver urn. It had been sent to Seattle in 1924 by the Emperor of Japan in gratitude for the funds sent by Issei to help Japan following a disastrous earthquake. We could not afford to purchase the urn but I learned that the rest of the material including lacquer sake cups which went with the urn had been sold to an antique store in La Connor, north of Seattle. Betty and I drove up that weekend and discovered a treasure. The crates contained material which had been housed in the Japanese Language School before the Evacuation. The crates were old ammunition boxes and had the name Genji Mihara on them. The crates contained text books, catalogues, the equivalent of two file drawers of written records and a few artifacts. At first we speculated that the crates had been disposed of by the language school but the presence of an expensive commemorative urn in the collection suggested that it was probably material seized by the FBI in 1942. The material was jumbled together in crates spilling their contents on the floor. We knew they contained information which needed to be preserved but could not afford to buy the entire collection. We did not speak or read Japanese so our sorting out of materials relied on intuition. After one hour Betty had to leave. The dust was too much for her. I kept working for another three hours. Each hour the store owner lowered his price. I finally could not resist. I told him to refasten the crates and ship them to the Astor Hotel. We loaded their contents on trestles in the Nippon Kan.

Eddie Harris and Tom Kaasa who worked at the University of Washington, both of whom read Japanese agreed to help sort out the materials. My secretary Keiko Foster was Japanese and she helped. Most of the books were textbooks from the prewar Japanese Language School but there was one classic, an illustrated copy of the "Forty-seven Ronin" published prior to Commodore Perry's opening of Japan. There were a few militaristic books which were rare. When McArthur governed Japan he had all such books in Japan destroyed. The hand written materials were from Seattle's pre war Japanese Association and included a 1924 census of all Japanese living in Washington, Montana, Idaho and Oregon. The census contained detailed information on families and businesses. It was funded by the Japanese government and conducted by the Seattle Japanese Chamber of Commerce. All of this was rich primary material for researchers of social history.

We offered to donate the materials to the University of Washington but they declined to accept the donation due to budget restraints. It took years before the importance of the material was realized. The University of Washington accepted the written records in 1980. A microfilm copy of the census was subsequently requested of the University of Washington for use by researchers at the University of Hiroshima, Japan.

Several paper wrapped wooden boxes, each containing a silk bound book, were also in our treasure trove. The boxes dated from 1924. These boxes were used as gifts and were important to many of the immigrants and their families who had finally realized that they would never return to live in Japan and were seeking to document their roots for their children. Each fold out book provided outlines for filling in family trees in addition to information on the number of Japanese in each state and other relevant material.

Family tree albums   60

Sagamiya Confectionary Store

When I first opened up my architectural practice I designed a building for Orville Cohen, a developer/contractor. His manager, Jim Kimbrough, called me one day and said that they were about to start work on a Senior Housing project and that the work would require demolition of an old wooden building located at S. Main Street and 6th Avenue South, the commercial heart of the old Nihon Machi. Jim had noticed some artifacts he thought I would be interested in and said I could have them if I retrieved them immediately. The building had housed Sagamiya Confection store founded by the Shibata family. The owner had sold special baked goods and decorative mochi for Japanese holidays. Mochi is made from a paste created by pounding rice using heavy wooden mallets. The paste is then hand molded into a variety of shapes. The Sagamiya baker had used a pile driving device which shook the whole building when it was in operation. I shudder to remember how he would insert his hand and turn over the paste between each stroke of the huge machine. He would then delicately shape the paste into chrysanthemum blossoms and other festive shapes. Pre WWII remains of the Maneki Restaurant were also in the building. My eldest daughter Linda and I raced down to explore. We found the old Tokuda Drug Store sign and several items related to the bakery and hauled them up the hill to the theatre.

We went back and climbed down into the basement. It had been designated as a potential shelter during the cold war years. Thank goodness it was never put in use for that purpose. It was a shambles. We waded through about four inches of what we hoped was water and discovered a barrel containing irons used for making senbei cookies. Senbei cookies have the same texture as fortune cookies but are not folded in shape. The batter is placed in iron molds with long handles and held over a fire to cook. This type of cookie is still being cooked in the lobby of the Kabuki-za Theatre in Tokyo.

Many of the flat molds had the name Shibata on one side and a design on the other. Several of the molds had the Alaska Yukon Exposition symbol on the other side. Others had the images of American Presidents all of whom had unusually slanted eyes. We assumed they were made in Japan for use at the Exposition. Other molds were in a variety of three dimensional shapes. One was of the God Hotei, another in the shape of a fox.

At the time of the Exposition, Japan was seeking trade with the United States and had a large pavilion located on the Exposition grounds where the University of Washington Forestry Building was subsequently built. The pavilion was not too far distant from the "Pay Streak" section of the grounds where restaurants and side shows were located. The Shibata family had operated Sagamiya prior to the Exposition and had a booth near the Exposition's Japanese Restaurant where they sold senbei cookies. We gathered all these irons and hauled them up the hill to the hall.

By this time Seattle's Museum of History and Industry had become aware that non Caucasians existed and their new director was augmenting their collection to reflect this. We donated the Shibata materials to the museum in the hope that they would add a replica of Sagamiya to their collection of old store fronts. My daughter still retains three of the irons as mementos of her basement odyssey.

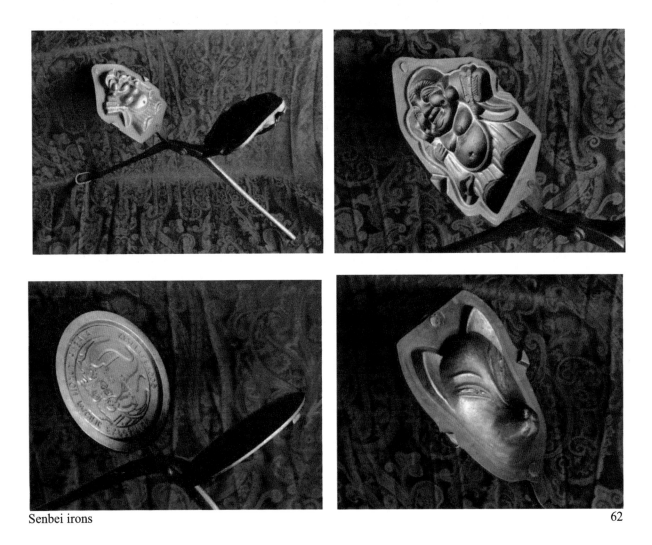

Senbei irons

62

Getting Hooked on History

Our first inquiries in the Japanese American community were met with reticence which we could not understand but which we respected and later understood. Intrigued, we visited Seattle's Museum of History and Industry and found only one book recognizing the existence of Japanese Americans in Seattle and no reference to the Evacuation. The University of Washington librarians helped but there was no category devoted to Japanese Americans. We discovered that recorded history is controlled by those who write it and by those who do or don't do the filing. Those who recorded Seattle's history did not want to remember the way Asian Americans had been treated. This was a rewriting of history by omission rather than the recent obfuscation attempts to rename slave ships as the "African Trade" and worse, recent changes in Texas text books to claim the existence of regiments of black soldiers in the Confederate Army when no such regiments ever existed.

My wife and I were disturbed by the omission of Asian Americans from Seattle's history and made a practice of reading books and other materials for references to Asian Americans. Kazuo Ito's "Issei" documenting the history of the early Japanese immigrants in the western hemisphere was a great find. Professor Carl Schmid's socio-geographic studies of Black, Japanese and Chinese residential movement patterns in Seattle proved fascinating. I also gleaned information from unusual sources. I found a photo of a Chinese cook in a display devoted to Scandinavian heritage. A book covering the building of the cross country railways had two pages devoted to the Chinese Americans who helped build them. All this gave us a clearer picture of Asian America history.

Chinese Cook   63

We collected aerial views and photos of Seattle and pored over them to find evidence of Asian American development. From these sources we developed a chronology of the vigorous and vital growth of an uninhibited frontier community in which Asians played a major role.

Friends provided what knowledge they had. Gradually, members of the Japanese American community began to share photos and memories. Largely because there had been no gathering of this history, Betty and I became known for our knowledge and became a focal point for those seeking information.

A Tour of the International District

My knowledge and interest in Seattle's Asian American history was of little use to my architectural practice but did open up another chapter in our lives. In 1974 I was asked by Betty Bowen, Director of Publicity at the Seattle Art Museum, to take her, David Ishii who owned a book store in Pioneer Square and a couple of other interested persons on a tour around the International District to share what I knew about the various communities it contained. We took off on a Saturday, toured the derelict Nippon Kan, visited the Sagamiya Confectionary Store on S. Main St., walked up S. King Street and had lunch together while I rattled on about the history of things we saw. Betty and David were impressed and she suggested privately that I make a practice of leading people through the district. She said I should develop a slide show covering the social history of the area. While I wanted to focus on my architectural practice I agreed that it was a story that needed telling.

Tour brochure   64A

Sheila Siobhan, the slide show 64B

I put together a twenty five minute slide show that showed the development of Seattle and the role of Asian Americans in that development, had a brochure printed at West Coast Printers and placed the brochures around town.

I offered a free tour to teachers as "in service" training. Seattle School District administration officials came first, were impressed and qualified the tour for use by Junior and High Schools. On the "in service" training day the turnout at my office was so large it had to be broken into several groups. Teachers found out that there were large gaps in their knowledge of Seattle history. Most had not heard of the Anti-Chinese riots or of the Evacuation.

The walking part of the tour included the Nippon Kan, Sagamiya Confectioners and S. Jackson Street up to the Chinese bulletin board, downstairs in Paul Woo's building to see fortune cookies being made by hand, upstairs to see an abandoned gambling den and ended in the Chinese bakery. We offered lunch packages in conjunction with Sun Ya Restaurant.

Diane Anderson with tour groups

65

As time went by, more people signed up for the tour and I had to rely on my secretary Diane Anderson and my daughter Sheila Siobhan to help out. Ultimately Betty took over the tours when she began managing the restored Nippon Kan Theatre. Over 40,000 students and an equal number of adults were introduced to Asian American history by the tour. We eventually had a Japanese language version of the slide show created for Japanese visitors. Junko Berberich and Midori Kono Thiel translated and narrated the tape.

We experienced some resentment from young community activists who knew nothing about the historic component of the tour and thought we were exploiting the residents of the District. We invited them to take the tour but they refused. We were considered "lofans", or outsiders. As a property owner I was an oppressing capitalist. Had they but known, the tour was never a money maker. It was ironic that one of the major themes of the tour was the problem created by racism.

We were urged to write a booklet providing the historical information contained in the slide show. This booklet titled "Seattle's Other History, Our Asian American Heritage" can be found in the Library of Congress, Harvard University, the University of Washington, the Wing Luke Asian Museum and other libraries throughout the United States. Today one can find scores of books written about the Asian American experience. At the time we wrote our booklet such books were nonexistent. An extract of this material is contained in Chapter 1 of this book.

Seattle's Other History Booklet   66

The Japanese Film Crew

One of the older photos we had of the Nippon Kan before the Evacuation was of a wedding. It was the only photo we had which showed the audience area of the hall. The hall was crowded with men seated at banquet tables. There were only two women in the photo, one of them the bride in full wedding regalia standing next to the groom. The other woman was holding a baby. Picture bride marriages were arranged by the immigrant's families in Japan. An immigrant would send his photo to his family in Japan and his family would arrange a marriage and send a photo of the prospective bride to him. If they agreed, the bride to be would come to America to be married.

1913 Fukuhara wedding   67A

Picture Brides   67B

We learned from Hosoe Kodama that not all of the men were honorable. Her husband to be had sent a photo taken when he was much younger. When he met her at the dock in Seattle, she refused to have anything to do with him. This took courage from a young woman who was facing a new unknown country on her own. She later married someone else and became an active and honored member of the community.

One particularly unlucky picture bride was Waka Yamada. When she arrived in Seattle she was forced into prostitution in one of the many brothels built on piling on S. Fifth Avenue east of the King Street Station. These brothels served the largely male immigrant community of Seattle. She fled to San Francisco where she was once again trapped. A social worker helped her and she married him. When he died she returned to Japan and became an acclaimed writer. She returned to the United States at the invitation of first lady Eleanor Roosevelt and when passing through Seattle gave a speech in the Nippon Kan. Many in the audience heckled her but were silenced when she said that she was the most qualified to tell of the hardships of women immigrants.

A Japanese film company produced a documentary of her life and asked me to assist in their research. I shared photos showing the area of the brothels and took them and the two stars that would play Waka on a tour. They were intrigued by Paul Woo's historic gambling facility and filmed many other sites in the district. They used accurate replicas of the Nippon Kan in the sets they used in Japan. We donated a video tape of the movie to the University of Washington in 1994.

OlderWakaactress studying historic photos.   68A

Younger Waka actress in the gambling den   68B

Filming Waka approaching Nippon Kan   68C

Chapter 5
Continuing the Heritage

Our decision to restore the Nippon Kan developed slowly but once in place we were open to any opportunity to accomplish the restoration.

The Center for Asian Arts

I was approached in the mid 70s by Professor Richard McKinnon from the Department of Asian Languages and Literature at the University of Washington. He produced a local newspaper covering Asian cultural events and was active in generating cultural exchanges with Japan. He had conceived a plan to develop an Asian cultural park with the Astor Hotel as its focal point. Traditional buildings would be transported from Korea, Japan and China to be located on the vacant land south of the Astor Hotel. We had no idea as to whether his claims of financial backing were real but were supportive of his efforts. We were fascinated by the story of his life.

Professor McKinnon's life had been a mirror image of the Japanese American experience following Pearl Harbor. He was Caucasian, born in Japan to American missionaries who lived in and had devoted their lives to Japan. He was not a Japanese American. He was an American Japanese. He was raised in Japanese culture and even attended a Japanese military school. He was in that school in 1942 when the Japanese bombed Pearl Harbor. The Japanese questioned his family's loyalty to Japan and he and his parents became outcasts from a land they loved and viewed as their own. They were deported, sailing on the Swedish ship S.S.Gripsholm, the last European ship to leave Japan. On his arrival in the United States he was conscripted into US intelligence because of his knowledge of Japan and his command of the language. He played a part in the US decision not to bomb Kyoto and was highly regarded in both the Japanese American community and in Japan.

We encouraged him and let him use two of the street level bays for the Center for Asian Arts free of rent. He held receptions and an art show consisting of prints by contemporary Japanese Artists. He also put on a calligraphy demonstration using famous calligraphers from Japan. In spite of his efforts it became obvious after time passed that his capacity to obtain funding to accomplish his dreams was not there. Regretfully we proceeded with a less ambitious plan.

Calligraphy demonstration   70

Official Recognition

We nominated the Nippon Kan for inclusion in the Washington State Register of Historic places. George Tsutakawa, an internationally renowned artist and member of the faculty at the University of Washington among other prominent members of the Japanese American community attended the hearing in Olympia and gave moving testimony in support of the nomination. The state commission decided unanimously that the Nippon Kan deserved to be on the National Register of Historic places in addition to the State Register and took action ensuring this would happen.

Hands on Improvements

I began a series of cosmetic improvements, planted trees on the south side of the building to match improvements being made by the city. I installed railroad ties at the edge of the gravel road and arranged bricks with my own hands between the street and sidewalk. I had to install the brick pavers twice as the first pavers installed were stolen. After I had acquired more bricks and laid them once again, the thief returned to take those bricks away. A vigilant neighbor in the adjacent senior housing called me and the police. The police caught him driving away with the loot. When I got to the building they were supervising the thief as he restored the bricks to their original location. The thief turned out to be a telephone worker who was stealing the bricks to improve his garden in Everett. He was bailed out and at his trial claimed he thought the bricks had fallen from the Astor Hotel. The judge told him that it was unlikely that the bricks would miraculously arrange themselves as pavers but gave him a suspended sentence with a stern warning.

Pre Restoration Events

In addition to the Center for Asian Arts use of the street level space adjacent to my office we had two uses of that area by outside groups one of which was a fund raiser. Franklin High School had a jazz band spearheaded by Chuck Chinn, an instructor at the school. One third of the enrollment at Franklin was Asian American. My daughter Allison played the flute in the band. Chuck arranged a tour of Europe for the group and fund raising was required. There were paper drives and other activities one of which was a reception party at the Astor Hotel. Abe Lum, a partner in the Chinatown Four Seas Restaurant had a boy in the band and he provided the food. It was a gourmet delight.

A lush banquet reception   71A   Allison Burke performs at Hing Hay Park   71B

Yet another group to use our space was the Norwegian Club of the University of Washington. My daughter Linda, president of the Scandinavian Club at the university had told folk about our unusual space. They decided to have their Christmas party complete with costumes and a Christmas tree with real candles burning in the branches. While the upper levels of the Astor Hotel were usually soggy from the rain, the wood was tinder dry. I kept my eye on the fire extinguisher.

| Playing with fire | 72A | Tanta Gubba distributes gifts | 72B |

We had been taking tour groups into the derelict hall but otherwise the hall could not be used because it did not meet building standards. In spite of this, with special permission, events did take place in the hall prior to its renovation.

Kobe Park

The City planned a park on land adjacent to the Astor Hotel and solicited names for the park. I suggested "Kobe Park" as Seattle was the sister city of Kobe, Japan and the park would be in the center of what had once been Seattle's Nihon Machi. The City did name it Kobe Park. The park design contained a sinuous path linking S. Main and S. Washington Streets and was filled with cherry trees. I vacated the street between the new park and our building and had the contractor who was building the park plant similar trees and ivy in the vacated street. We changed the name of our building to the 'Kobe Park Building'.

The City of Kobe Lantern

The City of Kobe Japan decided to contribute a large stone lantern to be located at the top of the park next to the Kobe Park building. One day an enormous Port of Seattle truck climbed our hill and several Kobe stonemasons started to unload the lantern. The load was so heavy it dented the recently installed street paving. It took several days to assemble the lantern.

Installing the Kobe Lantern   73A

Mayor Miyasaki of Kobe joined the stonemasons for the dedication ceremony. As Seattle's Mayor was out of town, Councilman Miller represented the City of Seattle. The Kobe-Seattle Committee was present composed mostly of Caucasian Japanophiles like myself. Professor McKinnon spoke and those at the dedication were invited into the gallery space he was then occupying in the Kobe Park Building. I also opened the Nippon Kan for a brief tour. Several of the Japanese stonemasons handed out packets of flower seeds as mementos of the event.

Mayor Miyasaki   73B

Councilman Miller   73C

I raised the carp banners on the flagpole donated by the Kobe Kiwanis Club each year thereafter in honor of "Boy's Week". I also climbed up the pole to untangle the carp when they wrapped around the pole much to the concern of my staff.

Kobe Park Festival

That summer the Japanese American communities celebrated the park with their own festival held on S. Washington Street adjacent to the Nippon Kan. It was not easy building food booths on the street due to the 15% grade but with many volunteers this was accomplished. The City of Seattle built a stage on the street. James Mason, city planner assigned to the International District, coordinated that portion of the work. Banners lined the street and the event was heavily attended. Councilman Sam Smith, Dave Towne from the Seattle Park Department and Tomio Moriguchi, President of Uwajimaya spoke at the celebration.

Early arrivals at Kobe Park Festival   74A

The Buddhist Temple Girls Drill Team   74B

Mrs. Moriguchi (lower right)   74C

Officials included Tomio Moriguchi, David Towne, Councilman   74D
Smith, Frank Hattori as MC and the Japanese Community Queen..

The Nippon Kan had been tidied up by members of International District Economic Association and under the supervision of members of the Fire Department the first traditional performances since the Evacuation in 1942 took place in the hall.

A Time to Remember

The only group willing to discuss the Evacuation in the early 1970s was the Japan American Citizens League. Issei and Nisei were even reluctant to discuss it with their children. Now this reluctance was diminishing. Min Masuda, a professor at the University of Washington, organized a community trip to Minedoka, Idaho, where most Seattle evacuees had been sent. He asked if he could hold a fund raising event in the Nippon Kan. The Fire Department gave reluctant permission contingent on the presence of at least three firemen to ensure that exits were accessible and that no smoking would be allowed. We tidied up and cleaned the hall as best we could and strung lighting with extension cords from my office space below. Those attending the event had to leave the hall at intermission time to use the toilets in my office downstairs. Min had arranged for folding chairs and a sound system. A large audience showed up. Speeches were given and traditional dance and martial arts were performed. One performer placed a potato on the stomach of a fellow performer, swung a samurai sword over his head and slashed the potato in two. We all gasped. Participants included Richard McKinnon, President of the Center for Asian Arts, Japanese Consul General Nishikawa and Mr. Kojima from JCS. Fujima Fujimine, Mrs. Takamura, Hitoshi Taniguchi, Midori Thiel and Hanayagi Yosono performed. A film clip from the National Japanese Television series 'Samurai no Tabiji' was shown. The setting was dreary but the enthusiasm of participants was great. The trip was a cathartic experience.

Samurai slashing a potato.   75A

Community dancers   75B

Year of the Dragon

In 1976 a group of Hollywood actors and writers visited the Nippon Kan. They included Mako, Pat Suzuki, Tina Chen and others. They held a reading of Frank Chin's play "A Time to Remember". Proceeds from this event were used to subsidize the trip to Minedoka. Once again the Seattle Fire Department was present to protect the audience.

Tazue Sasaki

1976 Sensei Tazue Sasaki with students   76

Sensei Tazue Sasaki who would later play a major role in restoring the heritage of the Japanese American culture to the Nippon Kan following its renovation held a private recital for her students in the derelict hall in 1976.

Chapter 6
Getting Under Way

We had placed a "for lease" sign on the building hoping for a tenant to come our way. The Seattle Indian Health Board indicated their interest and signed a lease as our major tenant. The State Office of Historic Preservation had advised us that we were eligible for a grant. All set to go, right? No.

At this point we were notified by City inspectors that the building's parapet should be reinforced. I faced jail time for failing to make the required correction immediately. I was brought before a judge who gave me a set period of time to make the required corrections. It was imperative to get the project underway.

We applied for a City Building Permit. Legally the Seattle Office of Historic Preservation had no jurisdiction over our project as we were not listed on the Seattle Register of Historic Places. In addition, Design Review Regulations for the International District specifically exempted the block we were on from design review. In spite of this, the director of the Seattle Office of Historic Preservation delayed approval of the permit for seven months for meetings with the local Design Review Board. He did this because he disagreed with my design approach even though the design conformed to State and National standards.

The design reflected an accepted approach; restore that which is historic but use contemporary materials for that which is not. I had planned a meticulous restoration of the historic sides to their original 1909 condition but on the blank north side I used 1980 materials. The city employee wanted the north elevation to be a Disney like imitation of 1910. While his job was to encourage historic preservation he almost killed our project. Given the inflation of that time his actions totally negated the benefit of the State grant.

Renovated east and south sides
78

When we finally had a Building Permit and a contractor's bid in hand we applied for financing.

We received a preliminary commitment from the bank but then, once again, the economy went haywire. Inflation soared, ultimately reaching 20%. The bank reneged on its commitment. (They actually used the word "reneging" in their letter). We despaired and considered leaving town. Knowing our plight an attorney told us that he had a wealthy client who might invest in the project if he could receive all of the tax benefits which came from investing in a historic building and be guaranteed a fixed cumulative return on his investment. To move the project forward we agreed to his terms. It was only following completion of the renovation and the renting of the building that we discovered that the agreement gave the investor not only all of the tax benefits but also all of the income from the building. It also produced an annual reduction in any benefit which we might have from a sale of the property.

Office space entrance   79A   Theatre entrance   79B

My office moved into a trailer parked in the adjacent lot and construction began. The work took over a year and was 20% over budget. I sold my house to help defray these expenses, borrowed from family and modified the building plans to include an apartment on the top floor that I would rent from the partnership for Betty and myself. It would be adjacent to and open into space I would rent for my architectural practice. My wife would rent the Nippon Kan Theatre from the partnership and would be on site to oversee events. All of our rents accrued to the benefit of our partner.

The Construction Process

Although the building had survived several earthquakes, it was not in compliance with current building codes. The walls and parapet structure required bracing. The floors needed to be securely tied to the outside walls with through wall bolts. Window frames had rotted and this had affected the stability of the bricks in which they were set so new reinforced concrete surrounds were required at all windows. All windows doors and frames needed replacement. While the floor structure could be saved the rotten flooring required replacing. All the brickwork, interior and exterior had to be pointed with mortar. A completely new electrical system was installed and connected to transformers in street vaults. To make the top two floors into flexible open office space the walls of the single rooms had to be removed and replaced with columns and beams. A new mezzanine was added to the top floor increasing the rentable space. Corridors leading to the offices were cantilevered from the north wall and an elevator was added. Air conditioning had to be installed. It was a major project.

Even before the Evacuation the Nippon Kan was in serious need of repair. The rosette lights surrounding the proscenium had been broken off. The plaster walls were rotting and portions of the ceiling had fallen. The flooring was warped and the antiquated electrical system needed complete replacement. Normal fire protection needs for a theatre were totally absent. The pigeons had to be removed.

On the other hand, the basic shape of the hall had remained intact. The audience area was a flat floor permitting very flexible use. The stage was relatively high affording good sight lines particularly from the balcony. Four columns intruded on the audience area but this turned into an advantage in the placement of chairs. The balcony at the rear of the hall was accessed by two stairs and the floor of the balcony was tiered. The musician's platform mounted above and to the right of the proscenium was intact. The theatre had a generous lobby accessed by a short flight of stairs from S. Washington Street. These assets were repaired and updated. An oak floor was installed in the audience area; a new softwood floor covered the old stage. Carpeting was installed in the lobby. Large fire exhaust vents were installed on the rear wall of the stage. The area under the stage was divided into fire retardant compartments. Fire sprinklers were installed. We developed a ticket booth in the lobby and a projection and lighting control alcove on the balcony. We developed toilet facilities accessed by a flight of stairs from the lobby.

We were unaware that the stage screen contained asbestos so we mounted it on the north wall so that new generations could see this piece of history. It was spaced from the wall to allow air circulation and had plastic over the lower portion to protect it from those using the hall. We also mounted plastic over the graffiti names in the stage wall to protect them. Having been erroneously assured that the building renovation was on budget we invested in stage equipment. This included blue velour stage curtains, a sound system, lighting and a lighting control box. I painted a pine tree in keeping with the Japanese theme on a cloth panel to conceal the sound speakers mounted just below the center of the proscenium. Acoustic panels were installed over the windows and on the rear wall of the house. Existing rosette light fixtures were restored and rewired.

Knowing from old photos of the hall that a great diversity of uses could be expected, we purchased stackable chairs and folding tables. We were ready to open the doors again.

Restored theatre, Betty giving tour slide lecture
81

Temporary Custodians of History

Following the restoration of the Nippon Kan, the Japanese government sent an official responsible for cultural affairs to find out what we were doing. He asked me how long I had lived in Japan. I told him I had never been to Japan. He thought for a moment and said "Then your wife must be Japanese". I replied "No, she has Scandinavian heritage". He was silent for some time obviously puzzled by the incongruity of our interest in Japanese history. There was no incongruity. Although events in the Nippon Kan prior to the Evacuation reflected the heritage of the Japanese immigrants, the hall provided a cultural bridge between the remembered past and the new American culture which the immigrants embraced. The Nippon Kan was part of American history. We wished to make this known.

Chapter 7
First Year, 1981

The first year was one in which the Japanese American and the broader Seattle community learned the quality and adaptability of the space, the excellent acoustics of the hall and the flexibility of Betty's management in making sure that users of the hall had a pleasant experience. In the first year Betty was always introduced as my wife. By the tenth year I was being introduced as Betty's husband.

The first event scheduled for the renovated Nippon Kan was the **wedding reception for Ann Cole and John Peugh** from Christian Community Church. Construction met with predictable delays. Betty, as future manager, grew concerned because of her promise of the space to the bride and groom. The work on the hall was prioritized and it was completely finished in time for the reception long before work was completed on the office space above. The couple wanted a unique setting for the reception. They got it. The hall was magnificent. The oak floor gleamed and the rosette ceiling lights cast a lovely pattern. The reception was highly successful and the chamber music players found out that the acoustics of the hall were excellent.

An intimate setting   82A

Perfect acoustics   82B

A starry ceiling   82C

Shortly after the first event in the hall we held an open house reaching out to the local community, in particular the Japanese American community. I baked cookies for the event using some of the senbei irons I had retrieved from the Sagamiya store. They were appreciated. Several elderly Japanese American women wrapped them in napkins and put them in their purses to take home. They were too precious to eat.

Strangely enough, the second rental of the restored hall was a Chinese event, a **Chinese Musical Instrument Demonstration and Sale**. The owner of Nordic House in Pioneer Square had originally had his Norwegian sweaters fabricated in Norway. He found that he could have identical sweaters produced in China for a fraction of the cost and established a working relationship with a Chinese company which also sold Chinese instruments. They wanted a demonstration performance in Seattle. Although he would have clearly understood the difference between a Norwegian and a Swedish person he was obviously not as clear on the difference between Chinese and Japanese. His Chinese event took place in the Nippon Kan.

Chinese instrument display   83

The first Japanese American event and the first wedding in the restored hall took place March 1st 1981. It was the **Debbie and Danny Uno Wedding & Reception**. The couple coincidentally had the same last name. Before the renovation, my very good friend Shigeko Uno, mother of the bride, had repeatedly asked if I would repair the rosette lights around the proscenium and in the ceiling. When she and I finally saw them restored and lit she remembered why they were important to her.

As a little girl she had been fascinated by the star like pattern they cast on the ceiling. She also remembered the hall as being much larger. Most of those who had been in the hall before the Evacuation had the same reaction. They had been small children at the time so the hall would have seemed very large to them.

March 3rd the Japan America Society of Washington State sponsored **Art of Kabuki**, a demonstration lecture by Leonard Pronko, Professor of Romance Languages, Pomona College. He and his Japanese assistant Takeo Tomono toured the west coast with a production demonstrating the art of Kabuki. He was a master and his contrast of the poses of a Japanese maiden as opposed to the poses of a Samurai was hilarious. The society sponsored Pronko's return in 1983.

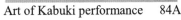

The Japan-America Society of the State of Washington
Presents

The World of Kabuki
by
Leonard C. Pronko
and
Takao Tomono
Thursday, October 13, 1983
Kilworth Chapel, University of Puget Sound
Friday, October 14, 1983
Nippon Kan Theatre, Seattle
Saturday, October 15, 1983
Nippon Kan Theatre, Seattle
All performances at 7:30 p.m.

Art of Kabuki performance   84A   84B

Our first play was produced by "Northwest Asian American Theatre". Bea Kiyohara, Director rented the hall for shows in April and May. The play was **Lady is Dying** written by Amy Sanbo and Lonny Kaneko. The cast included Fumi Ohashi, Frank Chin, Bea Kiyohara, Ted Shimazu, Maria Batayola and Sara Wilson.

Northwest Asian American Theatre Production   85A

In May we had our first rental of the hall for use by a group holding a meeting. The American Society of Landscape Architects rented the hall. After the meeting I took the group upstairs for a reception in my office.

Landscape Architects reception   85B

May also saw our first political fund raiser. Ruby Chow, a prominent leader in the Chinese American Community and future county commissioner placed her imprint of approval of Chinese American events in the hall by renting it herself.

When we redeveloped the Nippon Kan we were strongly advised by other facility managers not to rent the hall to dancers, martial arts groups or those putting on discos. Experience showed they caused a lot of damage. In the fourth month of operating the Nippon Kan, Betty was approached by members of the **Asian Student Association of the University of Washington**, most of them Sansei (third generation Japanese Americans), asking permission to rent the hall for a dance. We had rented the hall for a wedding reception that involved dance. Having a disco would be something else. Betty called and asked me to come down to the hall. She explained what the students wanted. I told them that protecting the hall was our highest priority so dances were not allowed. They said that the hall represented their history and their use of the hall was therefore very appropriate. They promised to protect the hall and offered a damage deposit. We relented but I told them that there was no need for a damage deposit as there would not be any damage. If damage occurred I would break their legs. They laughed but got the message. From that point forward the Nippon Kan was the scene of many happy dances by young Japanese Americans following in the footsteps of their parents. As time went on young Chinese Americans attended. Some were so young their parents dropped them off at the hall.

Aya Sakoda's Koto school held the first traditional music performance in the hall on May 16th. I must admit that my eyes were moist as I heard Sensei Sakoda play. She returned May 31st for another recital. When Aya was evacuated to Minedoka her Koto was confiscated. She bought a catalog Sears banjo, modified it and continued to practice during her internment. She returned each year for a performance with members of her school. On one occasion Aya called Betty to reserve the hall once again. After the call my wife realized that during the phone call she had inadvertently been bowing and saying "hai" in a Japanese expression of respect. Aya had a group picture taken after every performance in keeping with practice before the war. The photos themselves were very traditional with everyone looking grimly at the camera. Only after several uses of the hall was I able to cajole her into smiling for one of the photos. Sensei Sakoda later brought *Ikuta Ryu Chamber Music* performed by the Kyoto Todo Kai from Japan to the hall. Japanese performers included Shino and Elina Matsumura, Yasuko Tanaka, Kumi Takahashi and Tomoko Kurishi.

Aya Sakoda with students and Kyoto Todo Kai   86

With the **Sheila Siobhan Burke Recital** my daughter finally achieved her ambition to sing in the hall. Her coach for the concert was Susanne Szekely and her accompanist was Nancy Louise Cobbs. Sheila's program ended with a duet with her father. Ralph Rosinbum, a friend and professor in the opera program at the School of Music of the University of Washington was in the audience. After the recital he told me that my involvement was a nice touch but that in future I should leave the singing to Sheila. Sheila had many recitals in the hall after this first one. None contained duets. This concert made the excellent acoustics of the hall known to vocalists at the University. Since the hall had a flat floor and moveable chairs it was possible to arrange the main floor seating area to match the size of the audience. The hall felt comfortably full at all times even with a small turnout.

Sheila Siobhan on "Her very own stage" 87

In June, the International District Economic Association held a summer outdoor festival with an event in the Nippon Kan, **Flowers of Fire**, an evening of music, dance and poetry. Music was provided by the International District Band consisting of Deems Tsutakawa, piano, Marcus Tsutakawa, bass, Robert Antolin, sax and Harold White on the drums. Lonny Kaneko read his poetry. Ratna Roy performed East Indian dances and Takeo Yamashiro played the shakuhachi.

The International District Band   88

July brought the **Jim W. Johnson Recital**. When we obtained the six foot Steinway piano it needed breaking in. Betty let Jim try the piano out and based on his trial invited him to come to the hall anytime he wanted to practice. His playing was so forceful that we had to provide blocks behind the piano wheels to keep the piano in one spot. He played the first piano recital in the hall.

Each July Japanese Americans in Seattle hold the Bon Odori festival honoring ancestors. The Buddhist Temple opens its doors, food booths are erected and behind the church, restaurant seating is arranged on the parking lot. A large taiko drum platform is erected on the street fronting the temple from which an announcer directs dancers who form a single file in a loop in front of the platform.

Bon Odori Street Dance   89

Dancers come from all segments of the Japanese American communities and are augmented by Seattle Japan enthusiasts. All are dressed in traditional costume. My friend Shigeko urged me each year to join the dancers but in a rare show of shyness on my part, I declined. In 1981 the tradition of Bon Odori was augmented by the **Nippon Kan Bon Odori Disco** put on in subsequent years by Spank Inc. Young Japanese Americans and their friends came straight to the hall from the festival wearing their kimonos and danced to the latest disco music. The dance provided a wonderful blending of ancient custom with contemporary young people's activities.

August brought the **Tamura reception** and a **fund raiser for Charles Royer**, then running for Mayor of Seattle. The fund raiser was an Asian Cultural Pageant with performances from most of the Asian American groups in Seattle.

Katherine Collier Schotten, pianist and her husband Yizhak Schotten, violist, rented the hall in August for the Viola Club's **William Primrose Gala Concert.** The group had a packed house with most of the audience carrying violas. William Primrose, internationally known English violist was the featured guest. He pioneered use of the viola as a solo instrument and commissioned many original works by English composers such as Sir William Walton and Sir Ralph Vaughn Williams. On the night of the event, he was positioned in the center aisle in front of the stage throughout the performance. He apologized for not performing himself as he had discontinued playing professionally when he felt his skills diminishing. During the finale of the concert, all of the violists in the hall pulled out their instruments and he joyfully joined them playing with a hall full of thrilled performers. Maxine Cushing Gray, Editor of the magazine "Argus" gave the event a rave review.

In September Uslavi, a group of young musicians, rented the hall for a show called **The Banned Zone.** They hung a backdrop on the stage which strangely resembled the Nippon Kan before the renovation with broken bricks and peeling plaster. Their lighting was computer coordinated with the music and used all the flexibility of our stage lighting. Shortly into a trial of the system, the computer started to smoke and all thought of an innovative computer controlled lighting system was dropped. The lighting was controlled manually using our light board. The show went on and everyone except the computer programmer enjoyed it.

September saw a jazz show produced by Robert Antolin. He was the only performer to make use of the little musician's platform which was built over the right end of the stage.

On October 3rd the first use of the hall for films took place. The U.S. China Peoples Friendship Association and National Association of Chinese Americans had a showing of films.

When the upstairs construction was completed I held an opening reception for The Burke Associates, Architects. In honor of my deceased Scottish grandparents who raised me in my childhood in England, I hired a piper to play in full regalia. In November he brought the **Seattle Highland Games Committee Annual Party** to the hall. It withstood the acoustic and cultural trauma of marching pipers and drummers but my Scottish mother in law who watched from the balcony said that if she never attended another Scottish event it would be too soon. We were sure that the ghosts of prewar performers were turning in their graves.

Checking the door prize   91A   Scottish bagpipe serenade   91B

Offsetting this November cultural discord was a chamber music recital by the **Aeolia Ensemble** arranged by Richard Weeks, oboist and in early December the **Second Sheila Siobhan Burke Voice Recital** took place. Once again she was accompanied on the piano by Nancy Louise Cobbs. I did not sing.

December 5th saw the joyful return to the Nippon Kan of many of the Nisei who had been evacuated during WWII. George and Tama Tokuda brought the **C.O.H. Ai Iku Guild** to the Nippon Kan. George was a pharmacist. Tama had performed traditional dance in the Nippon Kan before the war. The event was a dance reunion with music and dances dating from their days in the camps. Jitterbugging and swing music bounced off the walls as middle aged Japanese Americans gaily swung their partners. I am afraid that the dance may have been a last hurrah in terms of jitterbugging for those in attendance. We were exhausted just watching them.

The next two weeks saw **Jazz at the Nippon Kan II** produced by Robert Antolin, the **Washington Jazz Society Show** with Woody Woodhouse, a **Christmas party** with a performance by Intiman Theatre sponsored by MacDonald, Hoague & Bayless Law Firm, a **movie** shown by the Coordination Council for North American Affairs with the Taiwanese Consul in attendance and the **Franklin High School Senior Dance.**
Heaven Can't Wait was a production by the young sansei members of the Japanese Presbyterian Church staged December 20th just before Christmas. Joyce

Bhang and Sharon Tekawa served as directors of the show which was an extravaganza based on the Christmas story but presented in Broadway musical form. Having angel heads peeking out through holes in a blue scrim while jiving with the shepherds below was priceless. It was gratifying to see a new generation of Japanese Americans following the traditions of their parents.

Bringing on the little ones   92

The **New Years Eve Disco** produced by Mint Productions rounded out the year and was the first of the annual New Year's Eve dances put on by this Japanese American group.

The first year use of the hall was less than expected but it did serve to make the hall's unique assets known to the broader Seattle community. We had seen weddings, receptions, parties, fund raisers, meetings, recitals, films, plays, jazz and classical music concerts, discos and one musical. It seemed that whenever we thought we had seen the ultimate use of the Nippon Kan someone would walk in with a different way of using it.

Chapter 8
The Nippon Kan Heritage Association

The Japanese Performing Arts Series

Betty and I had decided that we would not produce shows. We would rent the hall to groups and individuals. We would advise and help them with their productions but we would not initiate performances. We deviated from this policy in only one regard. We derived such enjoyment from seeing traditional Japanese performances by local artists in the hall during the first year that we decided to encourage them and attendance at them by sponsoring a Japanese Performing Arts Series. Our friend Tomio Moriguchi, produced fliers for three events. We posted them around the International District and crossed our fingers. The first concert in the series took place March 7th 1982. Yoko Gates, a highly respected koto player from Japan performed. Her friend Kimie West introduced us to her and Yoko agreed to kick off the series.

Tazue Sasaki.   93

The second event was a dance program by our friend Tazue Sasaki who performed under her professional name Fujima Fujimine.

The third event featured Kimie West playing the koto and Kodo Araki V playing the shakuhachi. Kimie was born in Japan and was an excellent Koto player. Araki lived on Beacon Hill teaching High School. His father and grandfather were professional performers in Japan and had been honored as Sacred Treasures for their skills. Kodo continued the tradition in the US but was finally persuaded much later by the Japanese Government to live and perform in Japan.

Kimie West and Kodo Araki V   94

The series was successful, covered most of its costs and received high praise from a local reviewer who was amazed that anyone would think to have such a series in Seattle. We needed a formal way of ensuring continuance of these events. I realized that I was oblivious to the competitive nature of some of those teaching traditional Japanese arts when sensei (honorable teacher) Takamura, a koto instructor visited my office with her daughter Marcia to find out why she had not been asked to play in our trial season. I needed help.

The Nippon Kan Heritage Association

I attended a grant writing seminar and that persuaded me to set up a nonprofit organization to continue the traditional arts programs. I gathered a small group which included Tazue Sasaki (Dance instructor) and her husband Yutaka (graphic designer), Midori Kono Thiel (artist and dancer), Joe Hirayama (business man) and Tama Tokuda who had danced in the hall before the Evacuation. Bill Taylor (Kabuki expert) and Deni Luna (media specialist) later joined with us. Tama reluctantly assumed the role of chairman on condition that I would remain active. The Board named the organization the Nippon Kan Heritage Association (NKHA). I applied for nonprofit status and we prevailed on Asian Multi Media to be an umbrella organization in applying for grants until we were certified by the IRS later in the year.

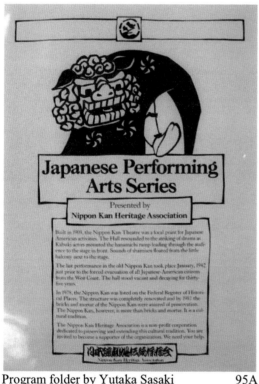

Program folder by Yutaka Sasaki   95A   Calligraphy designed by Yutaka Sasaki   95B

From that point on I printed and helped mail the fliers, Deni handled publicity. Midori performed at events and acted as master of ceremonies. She also took the lead in signing community performers up. Tazue acted as treasurer. Her husband Yutaka designed our program folder and built our stage screen. Joe Hirayama solicited advertisers for the program folder. We all joined together to sort out the announcements by zip code prior to each mailing.

September 22nd 1982 was the inaugural date for the series. Internationally known composer Alan Hovhaness played his compositions on the piano. His Japanese wife Hinako Fujihara sang and Frank Kowalski played the clarinet. There was the premier performance of "Sonata for Piano to Hiroshige's Cat" composed by Alan and dedicated to the Nippon Kan in honor of our cat.

Composer Alan Hovhaness and his wife Hinako.   96A

We were honored when he contacted us and were delighted to include him in the NKHA program. The day of the performance was my daughter Linda's birthday and she joined us in my office for a reception held after the event. We had a birthday cake and Frank Kowalski played "Happy Birthday" while everyone else including Hovhaness sang along.

Betty, Alan Hovhaness & George Tsutakawa   96B

Linda's birthday cake   96C

Alan returned in 1984 for a **Hovhaness Musical Evening** with his wife Hinako Fujihara and Daniel Shelhamer singing while Eileen Swanson played the viola. The "Campuan Sonata" was premiered. Alan became a good friend and gave additional recitals over the years.

The Nippon Kan Heritage Association averaged five productions a year not counting the visiting Japanese groups whose performances we facilitated. A few of these events are shown below.

Noh Dance, Midori Kono Thiel and Junko Berberich   97A

Urasenke Tea Ceremony   97B

Performer being costumed   97C

Hanayagi Yosono   98A

Betty, Tama Tokuda and Tazue Sasaki   98B

Under the aegis of the NKHA from its inception until our participation ended August 1990, Seattle was exposed to an impressive array of local traditional dance and music performers including: Fujimine Fujima's dance school; Aya Sakoda's Koto and Shamisen school; Bill Blauveldt and Seattle Taiko Drummers; Hanayagi Namisoto and students, Seattle Miyagi-Kai under the direction of Kuniko Takimura; Kimie West, koto; Kodo Araki V, shakuhachi; Hanayagi Yosono of Tokiwa-Kai; Junko Sakabe Berberich, singer; Midori Thiele, dancer; Hitoshi Tanaguchi, utai chanter; Bonnie Mitchell, tea ceremony expert; David Wheeler, shakuhachi; Takeo Yamashiro, shakuhachi; Teresa Kobayashi, koto; Yoshiko Kamo, dance; Katherine Mezur, dancer, Yoko Murao and Mary Ohno, dancers; Kinuku Shirane, koto; Naoka Noguchi, piano; Hiroko Muto soprano; Hansaburo Araki: Tani Sumi Hogaku, Kenkyu Group; Seiko Ogawa, Nobuko Ishida, Kasetsu Nakagawa, Kanami Onodera; Fujima Ohno and Kim Oswalt, koto. Many of these performers independently used the Nippon Kan for recitals.

Sensei Kuniko Takamura, Miyagi Kai   98C

Seattle Taiko Drummers   98D

Contemporary Works

The NKHA also brought innovative new works to the Nippon Kan. The **Deems Tsutakawa Quintet** played contemporary jazz in the hall.

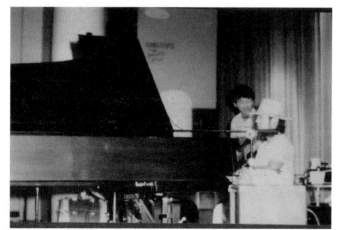

Deems and Marcus Tsutakawa   99A

Mailer for Esther Sugai concert   99B

In 1983 the NKHA also produced two shows of **Contemporary Works from Japan**. One was the **New Flute Ensemble** of Esther Sugai.

This was followed in 1985 by **Contemporary Japanese Music for Koto, Flute, Harp and Western Voice**. A premiere of *Rokudan Showa* by Jiro Senshu featured Naomi Kato, harp; Sheila Siobhan Burke, soprano; Trudy Sussman Antolin, flute and Kimie West, koto. In 1988 the NKHA produced **Music of the Tozai Ensemble** that included Kimie West, koto; Naoka Noguchi, piano; Paul Taub, flute; Hiroko Muto, soprano and Naomi Kato, harp. A blend of tradition and modern dance took place in 1987 with **Innovation and Change** produced by the *Japanese Fusion Dance Theatre of Katherine Mezur*. Yoko Murao used modern dance techniques while Mary Ohno performed using traditional techniques.

Paul Chihara

Paul Chihara composer   100A

Calligraphy by Yutaka Sasaki   100B

The NKHA commissioned music by Paul Chihara. He had worked in his parents' TV sales and repair shop on S. Jackson Street three blocks from the hall before going on to be nationally known in Hollywood and New York. King County had organized a major cultural event **Performa 87** and offered funding for new music and art. I persuaded Paul to write a new quartet, his *Serenade for Flute, viola, cello and harp*. He was reluctant because his memories of the Nihon Machi were not the best and he thought the Nippon Kan was still a derelict community hall.   The event featured his new quartet and other music he had written including the music for the film "Return to Manzanar" about the Evacuation. The film was shown and Paul gave a talk. Additional work was also played including his *string trio*, four songs from *Shogun* and his *Clarinet Quartet*. The Almont Ensemble and Felix Skowronek, flute, John Carrington, harp, Jeffrey Francis, tenor and Hiroku Muto, soprano performed.

Paul's mother died in a Seattle nursing home the night before the performance of his quartet and we were very worried that he would cancel. Fortunately he did not. After the performance members of the NKHA took him to eat in one of Seattle's finest Japanese restaurants, the Mikado on S. Jackson Street. We ate in a tatami room and I pointed out that he was sitting right where the cash register in his mother's shop had been located. He was very grateful that we had made the event happen.

Oshogatsu

Author as the Japanese Lion   101

Oshogatsu (New Year) is very special to the Japanese American community. Cleaning the house and paying debts before the holiday is mandatory. The first of each action must be performed to perfection. The NKHA produced an annual Oshogatsu show each year featuring dance, calligraphy, swordsmanship, poetry and other important aspects of the Japanese culture. During the first two years there was no one to perform the traditional Lion dance. Tazue cajoled me into taking on this role and coached me. I would dance onto the stage then fall asleep after scratching fleas with one of my legs. Tazue took the part of the butterfly teasing me awake and leading me off the stage into the audience where I received donations for the organization through the mouth of the lion. By the end I was soaked with perspiration but it was a lot of fun. One very old Issei lady came each year and took great delight in placing a dollar in the lion's mouth. I think I was chosen to be the lion because my Irish nature was well suited to idiotic frolicking and the soliciting of funds.

The dancer wears a black leotard under the lion's coat. I discovered that dance shops do not have much call for leotards fitting 55 year old men. When I first performed the dance, the cardiologist who had performed my open heart surgery six months earlier was in the audience to enjoy the show. His presence provided some reassurance for Betty.

Seattle had a treasure chest of performers committed to traditional and contemporary Japanese performing arts. The Nippon Kan Heritage Association provided access to this talent. Betty and I were deeply grateful to the members of the board who shared our vision and worked hard for years to accomplish these ambitious programs. They were good friends.

Chapter 9
Japanese Events

Akira Takeda was responsible for educational and social programs at the office of the Consulate-General of Japan in Seattle (CGOJ). He became a very good friend. In addition we became friends with the various Consuls who served in the CGOJ during the tenure of our involvement with the Nippon Kan. They were an invaluable resource in arranging Japanese performances. While the Consuls rotated every few years, Aki remained constant.

Shortly after renovation of the Nippon Kan was completed, the CGOJ sponsored the **Theatre of Yugen,** Noh and Kyogen performance on January 23rd 1982. There was no admission charge. Yuriko Doi was the director of the San Francisco based group. The group performed *Fukuro Yamabushi* (The Owl Mountain Priest), *The Sweet Poison* and *Three Handicapped Men* in English but with theatrical Japanese intonation.

As the audience left we heard several members conversing trying out English with Japanese intonation. It was hilarious. After the program we held a reception in our apartment upstairs. Akira looked at the sushi platters, did a quick calculation and said "But Mr. Burke, didn't the sushi cost more than the rent we paid?" It did.

The Theatre of Yugen returned the following year under the sponsorship of the Japan America Society. The Irish playwright Yeats had been fascinated by "Noh". The group performed an adaptation of his play *Purgatory* and also *Old Mountain Priest* and *Mistress Hang*.

In 1982 the CGOJ sponsored a group of young **Taiko drummers from San Francisco**. They performed the Lion Dance prowling through the audience.

San Francisco Taiko　　　　104A

The **Nomura Kyogen and Noh** performance was sponsored by the Seattle Art Museum with the cooperation of the CGOJ. The performers descended from a long line of Kyogen performers and were national treasures of Japan.

Kyogen Performance　　　　104B

Noh Performance   105A

Because of support from the Seattle Trust Guest Artists Program there was no admission charge. Even so, we urged Sonnet Takahisa, the museum's coordinator, to issue tickets. The museum didn't. On the day of the event the line of people waiting to get in was over a block long and wove through the adjacent parking lot. The maximum legal capacity of the hall was 399. We counted back in the line and advised all those after that point that they could not get in so there was no use waiting. Not all of them left. My wife Betty guarded the door with an old railway counter and ensured that only 399 were admitted. Many of our friends and a newspaper event reviewer could not get in much to our chagrin.

Line up for Kyogen event   105B

Akira also assisted the **Kobe Chamber Orchestra** when it visited Seattle in 1982 and performed two weekends. Their visit was sponsored by the Seattle Kobe Affiliation Committee and the Japan America Society. Ryutaro Iwabuchi, the conductor was used to conducting on a podium. The group's manager had limited English but with sign language was able to convey his needs. They rehearsed while I banged a podium together with scrap wood. The conductor needed to rest so we took him upstairs to our leather lounge chair. Our cat nestled in his arms and they both napped. I decided the podium looked a little raw so I put a fast coat of shellac on it. Unfortunately it was still tacky during the performance and the conductor's shoes made squeaking noises. He was a good sport and laughed about it later. Before their next performance I was able to cover the shellac with fabric. He was grateful. The orchestra performed works by Mozart, Britten, Akutagawa and Tchaikovsky. At the completion of their playing of Schoenberg's "*Transfigured Night*" there was silence in the hall for several seconds. The audience was so enthralled they did not want to break the mood with applause. I have only experienced this response twice in my lifetime. Mary Fain of the Seattle Times wrote "Magic, pure Magic". The conductor assumed this was a political courtesy. We told him it was not.

Performance of Kobe Chamber Orchestra   106

The Kobe Deputy Mayor and a delegation of 100 Kobe citizens came to Seattle with the orchestra. It was the 25th anniversary of the Sister City Agreement. We held a reception for the delegation in my office. The men in the delegation were standing around a model of Highway I 90, a project my office was working on but their wives were all standing along one wall looking bored. I took them into our adjacent apartment. They were fascinated by the size of our refrigerator and especially by its ice dispenser.

Newspaper and magazine articles in Japan reported on the Nippon Kan in glowing terms. Performers planning tours in the United States made a point of making the Nippon Kan one of their venues. Our problem was that we were many times unaware of the quality of the performers. One of these was the **East Comes West** concert facilitated by Akira at the CGOJ and sponsored by the Japan America Society and the NKHA. John Kaizan Neptune, an internationally known performer on the Shakuhachi but unknown to us led the quartet. The show was fantastic. The audience was adequate but could have been bigger had we known. The next day we purchased one of his records at a music store. The checkout clerk was dismayed that he had missed the one live performance ever to take place in Seattle.

Hozan Yamamoto
107

Ondekoza Demon Drummers   108A

The **Ondekoza Demon Drummers** almost brought the hall down. Just prior to their show, Seattle Junior Theatre had produced "Anna and the White Crane", a play for children which had a scene with falling snow created with small pieces of white paper released from the stage ceiling. Residual snowflakes fell during the Ondekoza performances. We were afraid plaster would crack and fall from the walls. The group had a drum carved out of a huge tree trunk. They had no English and it was difficult to explain that they could not position their giant drum in front of one of the emergency exit doors. We had to remove all evidence of demons prior to use of the theatre by an evangelist group the following day.

Mary Ohno   108B

In 1984 and1985 the CGOJ sponsored programs produced by **Mary Ohno**, a recent arrival in the United States. She danced, played Japanese instruments but also strange to tell she played the ukulele. She stayed in Seattle and used the Nippon Kan many times for her own recitals. She also performed in NKHA events.

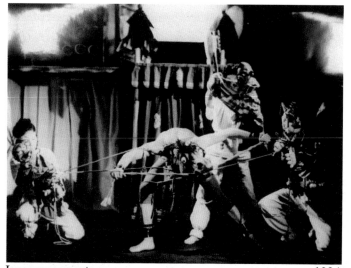

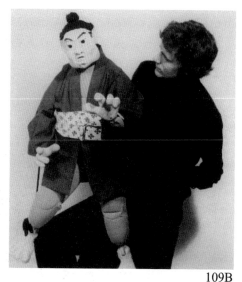

Japanese puppeteers   109A   109B

The CGOJ helped bring in the **Japanese Puppet Theatre** produced by *Deaf Puppet Theatre, Hitomi-za*. The show was sponsored by the NKHA. They presented *Hands and Faces* and *Tono Story*. Tono Story was a trifle risqué as it is based on a folk tale of the Tohoku area of Japan about a stallion and the village chieftain's daughter. I am not sure that the young members of the audience were aware that consensual sex between the stallion and the maiden was part of the story. After the show it was fascinating watching the performers interacting with deaf mute members of the audience. Sign language transcended the normal language differences.

In 1985 The Tateyama Shirayuri Orchestra came to the hall. It was a Youth Senior Orchestra having their first exposure to the United States.

The programs described above are just a few of the cultural exchange events which received assistance from the CGOJ. Akira Takeda did not know it but as far as the NKHA was concerned he was an honorary member of the Board.

Chapter 10
Pioneering Contemporary Music

For ten years the Nippon Kan served as the home for most of the contemporary classic music concerts which took place in Seattle. Our family adopted a new expression "Betty's Music" to reflect her management during this period. Four major institutions pioneered contemporary music in the Nippon Kan. They were the Seattle Symphony Orchestra led by Gerard Schwarz; Marzena led by Bob Priest; the Washington Composers Forum and Soundworks. These four were augmented by a host of other performers who brought new music to the ears of Seattleites by performing in the Nippon Kan. The four groups gained energy from each other and stimulated the creation and performance of new music in the northwest.

King County's **Performa 87** and the **Goodwill Games** provided a financial boost for this burst of musical energy supplementing the ongoing support provided by other governmental organizations and private foundations. The Nippon Kan provided a venue in which this musical renaissance could take place.

The Seattle Symphony Orchestra

The Seattle Symphony Orchestra had performed in the Nippon Kan prior to the Evacuation. We had recognized Ronald Phillips, then the Seattle Symphony's first chair clarinetist, as one of the players in the Miyashita photo we had enlarged and mounted in the lobby of the Nippon Kan and had invited him to see the restored hall. He identified all 24 of the players, eight of whom were still active at that time. Ronald pulled his clarinet out of its case and played opening notes from Gershwin's "Rhapsody in Blue", much to the delight of our cat that was prowling the hall at the time.

In 1985, Gerard Schwarz, conductor, produced the "New Music Series". The size of the Nippon Kan was perfect for his programs. For a five year period the

Symphony performed in the hall once again. Each year the Symphony had a composer in residence and we were fortunate to meet well known composers such as John Corigliano, Stephen Albert, Roger Bouland and George Perle among others. A description of the events is contained in the appendix.

Seattle Symphony Season Flier   111

It was a great pleasure to hear the interaction of Schwarz, the composers and the orchestra players however not all the interaction was subtle. While one piece was being rehearsed in the hall an orchestra player asked "what expression is required by the piece?" The composer replied "Just play loud". It would be impolite to give the composer's name.

Preparation space was not a problem for the orchestra. They spread their instrument cases and coats throughout my office upstairs and in our apartment Betty always provided snacks and soda. Schwarz commandeered the leather reclining chair in our living room as he prepped for the concert. The Nippon Kan was accessed down our exit stairway.

Symphony performers applauded by Gerry Schwarz.   112A

One performance started with a horn entrance line. The orchestra came on stage, followed by Schwarz. He raised his baton only to find that the horn player was not present. Apparently traffic was heavy on Highway I-90 making him late. The piece was moved to later in the program.

One horn player missing   112B

Many of the orchestra members used the hall to perform individual recitals and played in concerts with the other new music groups. We found that the musicians of Seattle were strong supporters of each other.

For most events in the theatre we were able to use our stage lighting. The Symphony however had strict rules requiring bright lighting and dealt with a strong stage hands union. Whereas I could normally adjust the stage lighting for a group using the theatre in just one hour, the orchestra's union required a half day and five of their stage hands to do the work. They brought in and set up their own lights then sat in the lobby while the musicians played. The stage hands did not like new music.

Marzena

Bob Priest inaugurated the Marzena new music series in 1986. Bob had recently returned to Seattle from Poland and was enthused about the concept of combining art forms for events. He engaged artists to design stage sets and floral arrangements and invited composers at the cutting edge of new music around the world to come and have their pieces performed. In subsequent years he cooperated with the Seattle Symphony and when they had composers visit Seattle he would allocate a concert in the Nippon Kan for their work. Bob staged twenty eight performances in the Nippon Kan featuring innovative new work by over sixty composers.

His events were very eclectic. One of his programs was *Other Works by Strange People with Foreign Names.* Another program consisted of a panel of experts discussing *Yes, but is it Music?* Bob's creative juxtaposition of actors, musicians, artists and dancers in his programs made each event truly eventful. Betty shared with Bob one of the secrets of a successful concert: advertise free refreshments and the audience will come. The Nippon Kan setting provided an additional benefit to concert goers. At intermission time they would cross S. Washington Street from the theatre to browse on the wild blackberry bushes growing on the adjacent vacant property.

Marzena poster   113

Washington Composers Forum (later NW Composers Alliance)

Seattle had a lively community of composers who had formed an association to produce concerts of their work. Their music was so far "out" that their audiences were very small. The Nippon Kan was perfect for their needs.

The first program opened with Karen Thomas' *Cowboy Songs*. The cellist Walter Grey came on stage wearing a cowboy hat, jeans and neckerchief. He played with the cello resting on his knees like a guitar while he sang the lyrics. It was hilarious and more. It was an excellent piece of music. As she left the hall I bent over and whispered in her ear how much I enjoyed the work. Betty was appalled. She thought I had kissed Karen on the cheek. That would not have been very professional. Karen had several pieces premiered in the hall under the aegis of Composers Forum and went on to be a leading light in Seattle's music scene.

Composers on the faculty of the University of Washington such as Stuart Dempster and Diane Thome participated in these concerts. Stuart performed one of his pieces for trombone with a flashlight on the instrument so he could play his composition while walking through the audience in the darkened hall.

One of the forum's younger members was called Mahler. Though he was no relative of the renowned Austrian, he was a very fine musician and introduced us to minimalist music. I had the contract to provide planning services to Washington State University east of the Cascade Mountains and Betty would sometimes drive me there. On one five hour drive she played a tape of his music over and over again until I finally understood what minimalist music was all about.

He puzzled his fellow musicians at one concert by playing extremely atonal music on a reel to reel tape machine and singing along with it. It was a spoof. Half way through his performance he reversed direction on the machine. When the tape was played correctly we learned that he had been singing and playing the national anthem backwards.

Program Announcement 115

Soundworks

Soundworks was the first group to consistently produce events featuring new music in the Nippon Kan. Their performances ran from December of 1984 through July of 1990 and included electronic music, music for newly invented instruments in addition to music in which the sounds of standard instruments were modified.

For one concert the composer asked to modify the hall's Steinway piano to achieve special sounds. Betty defended the Nippon Kan's piano fiercely but for this occasion she allowed her own piano tuner to make adjustments before and after the concert.

In 1987 Soundworks transitioned to a new organization *Earshot Jazz*. Herb Levy was directly involved with producing in both groups.

In 1990 Soundworks took advantage of the **Goodwill Games** funding to put on an *International Computer Music Festival*. Six events filled with new music provided a broad range of work.

Chapter 11
Noteworthy or Frequent Hall Events

The National Flute Society Convention August 1982

Felix Skowronek, a member of the music faculty of the University of Washington, was a member of a woodwind group which performed in the restored Nippon Kan. He subsequently acted as coordinator for the Annual Convention of the National Flute Society held in Seattle and booked several of its events into the Nippon Kan. The Tokyo Flute ensemble filled the stage and performed orchestral works with a wide variety of flute instruments some as big as tubas. Stephen Preston performed and gave an insightful talk on the history of the flute. One of these events featured Julius Baker whose performance attracted James Galway and his entourage. They filled the front row of the balcony.

Stephen Preston   116A

Tokyo Flute Ensemble Signatures   116B

Horrortorio and the Tale of the Thing

This 1987 performance by Philharmonia NW and the NW Boys' choir took place using a Halloween theme. The names, costumes and grotesque make-up of performers were in keeping. The Forest Lawn (cemetery) Philharmoania (not misspelled) Orchestra was under the direction of Maestro Joseph Crnko. Soloists included Marjorie Sacket, strangler soprano, Ann Wickstrom, morbid mezzo, Jon Palmason, torture tenor, Don Collins, butcher bass and Mak Hoover, continuo. Lyrics of the musical selections were modified to reflect the theme. During one of the pieces performed, the heads of choir members protruded from a huge orange sheet stretched over the stage. Adding to the gruesome effect, one of the boys became sick and vomited before slipping down beneath the sheet. At the end of the piece the stage curtains were drawn and he was retrieved safe and sound. The show went on.

Halloween at its worst   117

Finlandia Foundation

The first event was fairly straight forward. The Academic Male Voice Choir of the Helsinki University of Technology under the direction of Hack Saari sang in the hall to an appreciative audience. A Karonkka (party) followed.

The second performance was different. Betty was not present when a huge bus climbed the hill and disgorged thirty two dancers, ten singers and five musicians. They were the Tanhuajat Finnish Folk dancers for the **Turun Kansantaznssin**

Ystsavat concert. They had booked assuming that they would first go to home stays with members of the Finnish community to prepare for the event. Time did not permit this so they showed up at the hall. They needed to prepare their costumes, clean up and prepare for the evening. The Nippon Kan had no dressing rooms so there was no other option than to let them use our apartment and my office space for their preparations. Fortunately it was a Saturday so none of my employees were present. Our washing machine ran continuously. All forty-seven of them took turns disrobing and ironing their costumes in our dining room. It was a great surprise for Betty when she came home.

Mayhem in our apartment   118A

Finns galore   118B

The concert was a smashing success. Finland is a northern nation and the folk dances are lively to keep the dancers warm. The audience was primarily Finnish American, many of whom were due to house the dancers for the night. When the program was over the dancers came off the stage, chairs were pushed back and everyone danced. It was rollicking good fun.

Finnish folk dancers and musicians   **118C**

The Way It Was Exhibit

In 1985 the NKHA organized *The Way it Was: Northwest Issei and Nisei Before 1942,* an exhibit of life in the Nihon Machi before WWII. It focused on the happy times before the Evacuation. Ryo Tsai acted as librarian with Hideo Hoshide and Harry Fujida doing much of the fund raising and leg work. Tama Tokuda our dear friend was a member of the group. Photos were displayed on free standing moveable racks set around the audience area of the Nippon Kan. For legal reasons we charged rent: one dollar for the year. Our diverse audiences were fascinated. We stored the exhibit during discos and other events. A calendar containing some of the photos in the exhibit was produced by Mrs. Tsai. It sold out almost immediately. While the show was on display I urged the group to have a duplicate of the material placed in the University of Washington Library. I was unsuccessful. It would have been a good addition to the documented history of Seattle. I have recently learned that the daughter of Mrs. Tsai has donated the photos and slides from the exhibit to the Wing Luke Asian Museum. They are a treasure.

Calendar

Music for Flute by Contemporary Composers

Paul Taub, flutist, organized this event bringing Nicolas Slonimski, an American composer to hear his work played together with work by a namesake Russian called Mikhailovich Slonimski.

Nicolas Slonimski (born in 1884) maintained a monumental encyclopedia of music for many years. It covered who's who and what they are doing in the music world. His work "Quaquavers Suite for Flute, Piano & percussion" was premiered at this event. Its movements were: Square Root of Beethoven's Fifth; Gypsy Russian Song; Anatomy of Melancholy (with cat); Big Loud Tone Clusters Alternating with Soft Chords; Interplay of Two Mutually Exclusive Scales; Typographic Games (black & White with Regular Typewriter) and Bitonal Scale for Birds.

Mikhailovich Slonimski (born 1932) wrote "Recitative, Aria e Burlesca" dedicated to Paul Taub. It was premiered at the event. The concert also included works by Gubaidaluna, Nagovitsin, Vasks, Gabeli and Taktakshvili. The performers were Paul Taub, flute, Roger Nelson, piano, Mathew Kocmieroski, percussion, Rachel Swerdlow, viola and Pamela Vokolek, harp.

Forty years earlier Betty had climbed trees in Boston with Nicolas' daughter Electra. She met her once again while attending Nicolas' lecture/discussion at Elliot Bay Bookstore. It is a small world.

Dances and Songs from the Silk Road

On the morning of November 20th 1982 Betty was contacted by the Seattle/Chun Qing Sister City Association to reserve the Nippon Kan for an event to take place that evening. Five musicians and two dancers had unexpectedly arrived in Seattle to perform the "Dances and Songs from the Silk Road Ballet" and needed a venue. There had been no opportunity to send out publicity so we were highly skeptical about the ability to muster an audience. We should not have worried. Somehow the word passed quickly through the Chinese American Community and the show had a packed house.

Japanese Culture Festival

This event was arranged by Stacy Higiya of Simply Desserts and was similar to a street fair but indoors. Booths were set up on the audience floor and artisans demonstrated their skills. Artwork was displayed in the lobby of the hall. Bonsai tree growers demonstrated their craft and sold plants. A calligrapher demonstrated and sold examples of her work. Weavers and potters also participated. At one point in the event there were traditional Japanese performances on the stage.

121B

121A

Arts and crafts fair in the Nippon Kan   121C

121D

Bar Mitzvah

When Norm Sandler a fellow architect's son came of age he asked if he could hold the bar mitzvah party in the Nippon Kan. He thought it was a unique space and it was. He then hired a party consultant who completely changed it into a circus atmosphere. Large papier-mâché animals were set in the lobby. In a nod to tradition, two separate food serving stations were set up between the theatre's four columns. A disc jockey was positioned on the stage. One of the food prep stations cooked hamburgers and hot dogs while the other prepared desserts customized for the kids attending the party.

It was a costume party and parents of the kids at the event had obviously spent a lot of energy to make their kids unique, but it was Norm's best friend who was the most creative. He was similar to Norm in height, weight and physical attributes. He had his hair styled as a frizzy afro identical in color, shape and texture to Norm's hair. His costume matched. It was hard to tell them apart. It was a complete surprise to Norm.

Bar Mitzva 122A

Asian Culinary Art 122B

Seattle Art Museum Asian Arts Council

The Council used the hall on several occasions. One was a party with a Chinese theme. Another was a culinary and a calligraphy demonstration. George Tsutakawa, an internationally recognized sculptor and painter and his wife Ayame chaired this event. The culinary part of the program was messy and following the show George found a brush and began sweeping the floor. I told him it was a terrible misuse of his brushwork technique.

Plays
Northwest Asian American Theatre (The Asian Exclusion Act)

The "Asian Multi-Media" group was developed to assist young Asian Americans interested in various art forms. Frank Fujii, artist and a teacher at Franklin High School was an instigator of the program which enabled a sharing and honing of skills in a multi-discipline environment. Several of those who benefited from Frank's work were interested in writing, acting and design of stage productions. Frustrated in their efforts to get a foothold in their field they formed the "Northwest Asian American Theatre" (NWAAT) under the leadership of Bea Kiyohara. Once the Nippon Kan was renovated NWAAT was able to produce *Lady is Dying* in the first year.

The second production was *F.O.B.* (an abbreviation for "**F**reight **O**n **B**oard" but in this case an abbreviation for "**F**resh **O**ff the **B**oat"). The play ran for a full month. The play was written by David Henry Hwang. Jill Chan played Grace, Greg Hashimoto played Dale and Christopher Wong played Steve. Judy Nihei directed the production.

NWAAT poster   123

The group initiated *Community Show Off* a satirical production with leading community activists spoofing politicos and their programs. Social activists such as Bob Santos, Larry Gosset, Roberto Maestas and Bernie Whitebear performed. The show became an annual opportunity to let off steam.

A *Song for a Nisei Fisherman* was the next NWAAT show. Written by Philip Kan Gotanda it was directed by Denise Ford. Carmine Simone handled the lights and Silas Morse designed and built the sets.

1984 brought two staged readings. *Benny Hana* by Amy Sanbo and Lonny Kaneko with Denise Ford directing and *The Romance of Magno Rubio,* Carlos Bulosan's short story adapted by Nancy Rebuilt and directed by Maria Bataloya.

Yellow Fever by R.A.Shiomi ran for one week in May. This was followed by *InnovAsian '84* directed by Marian Bengie Santos, Director and Choreographer in July and in November *Flowers and Household Gods* by Momoko Iko.

NWAAT posters   124A   124B

Gathering Ground, We Cannot Wait to be Discovered was produced by NWAAT in 1985. The program consisted of poetry, drama, song and dance. Maria Batayola directed.

Breaking the Silence written by Nikkii Louise was produced in 1986. Mifsud directed the show with a cast including Harry Fujida, Gregg Hashimoto, Fumi Higashi, Leslie Ishii, Bea Kiyohara, Richard Lewis and Jan Locke.

Mother Goose Theatre

The focus of this group was the production of plays suitable for an audience of children. Most productions took place during the daytime and attracted school groups. *Raggedy Ann in Candyland* was a typical production.

Other Productions

The Last of the Red Hot Lovers by Neil Simon was a three night production of Café Theatre, Lincoln Arts.

Posters   125A   125B

Ama and the White Crane was presented by Seattle Junior Theatre. One scene was a snowscape. Small white pieces of paper were released gradually from bags mounted on the stage ceiling light bars creating a highly effective image of snow falling.

The Serpent Within Me was produced by Sasa Havi of Collective Spirit Theatre. This was the Nippon Kan's only American Indian production.

El Centro de la Raza presented *Fire from the Mountain*. John Gilbert, actor and Peggy Sheen and Friends were the performers. Comandante Omar Cabezas, Vice Minister of the Interior, Republic of Nicaragua spoke. He had four Nicaraguan army bodyguards with him, all with their arms tucked in their long coats. During his speech two of them stood on either side of the proscenium watching the audience, two of them stood in the lobby guarding the doorway. We assumed the comandante had enemies. A subsequent program was produced by the Seattle-Managua Sister City association in which Francisco Campbell, Minister Counselor for Political Affairs with the Nicaraguan Embassy spoke. He had no bodyguards in evidence. The Total Experience Gospel Choir performed at that event.

Films

During the first year following the renovation the Japan America Society used the hall to show a documentary film on Japan. They held similar events each year thereafter.

In 1985 the movie *Beacon Hill Boys* was shown. It was produced in cooperation with King Street Media and Evergreen State College. Immediately following WWII Beacon Hill was the neighborhood in Seattle in which Asian Americans could find homes to rent or buy. The movie was about the problems of the younger generation living there. Dean Hayasaka, Ken Mochizuki and Bill Blauvelt were co-producers. Performers included young and old Chinese and Japanese Americans representative of the Beacon Hill neighborhood. They were Ken Mochizuki, Christopher Wong, Gregg Hashimoto, Ed Lock, Nonie Tao, Jodie Tanino, Tama Tokuda, Frank Kaino, Fumi Higashi, Harry Tate, Frank Fujii, Arnold Mukai, Ron Howard and Bea Kiyohara. Also shown at this event was *Fools Dance* by Bob Nakamura featuring Mako, a Hollywood star. Both movies were premieres and ran three nights.

That same month *Unfinished Business* by Steven Okazaki was shown. It was a film about three men who resisted the Evacuation. The event was sponsored by the Japanese American Citizens League as a benefit for the Gordon Hirabayashi Defense Fund.

Several of those involved in the above productions presented the *First Seattle Asian American Film Festival.* Films included Only Language He Knows; Chan is Missing; The Silence; The Serving Woman and Hito Hata.

In 1986 *East of Occidental* was shown.

Through the years many films were shown in the Nippon Kan most of them educational productions sponsored by a variety of groups such as the Japan America Society.

Orchestral Use of the Nippon Kan

In addition to the Seattle Symphony, Seattle had many other orchestral groups all producing great music in the Nippon Kan.

In 1985 The Thalia Chamber Orchestra played under the baton of Francis Walton. In 1986 the orchestra played "The Story of Babar" in March then returned in May and November under the direction of Roupen Shakarian. The orchestra became a regular user of the hall.

In 1987 the Philharmonia Northwest played the first of many concerts. In 1988 the orchestra premiered Shakarian's Symphony No 1. The orchestra returned later in the year and in the following years up to 1990. Soloists included Julie Sigars, soprano, Cathy Ledbetter-Taylor, oboe.

December saw the advent of elaborate performances by the Northwest Chamber Orchestra using the theme "Court of Louis XIV". Works by Lully, Charpentier, de Llande, Corelli and Campora were played under the direction of Dr. James Savage. Nancy Zylstra, Louise Marley, Paul Karatis and Norman Smith augmented the orchestra. The stage was decorated in accordance with that period. A beautiful gilded Christmas tree sat to the edge of the proscenium. The group offered to leave the tree in the hall but unfortunately the religious group using the hall the next day disapproved. The tree had to go. The group produced a similar event in 1988 titled "Royal Holidays in Versailles" playing a piece using a glass harmonica invented by Benjamin Franklin. A swing was placed front and center on the stage and actress Diane Schenker acting the role of Marie Antoinette swung over the heads of the audience sitting in the front row. In 1989 the show was titled "Royal Holidays in Versailles, The Court of Napoleon III and Empress Eugenia". Jeff Francis, Louise Marley, Norman Smith and Nancy Zylstra sang. Diane Schenker also performed. These productions became so popular that they had to move to a larger hall, Saint James Cathedral.

Recital Performers and Chamber Groups

The hall provided a cozy ambience for soloist recitals and chamber music groups playing everything from medieval to modern music. Music recitals were the bread and butter of the Nippon Kan's use. A list of events is contained in the appendix.

Weddings

Our first event in the Nippon Kan following the renovation was a wedding reception. This was followed by forty one weddings or receptions a few of which are described below. All are listed in the appendix.

The wedding of Tom Ikeda and Sarah Yamasaki was unique. Her father Frank arranged to have the hall and stage densely lined with large fir trees. He hung lights from the front edge of the balcony shining down on the wedding cake below. We held our breath during the ceremony when the cake began to melt.

A Buddhist wedding was conducted by a priest next to the lantern in Kobe Park with the reception following in the Nippon Kan. A mentally challenged man wandered by and I did some fast talking to keep him quiet during the ceremony. A muscular Nisei was in the wedding party. He thanked me saying that if persuasion had not been effective he would have helped me physically remove the intruder. I have forgotten the name of the Nisei but remember that he showed me that he was in a group of sumo students contained in a picture hanging in the theatre lobby.

Wedding reception   128A

Deems Tsutakawa on the piano   128B

My daughter Sheila Siobhan was married in the theatre. Her husband William Lewis had performed for thirty years at the NY Metropolitan Opera Company and in major cities around the world. His best man was Gordon Getty Jr., the oil magnate/composer who flew up from San Francisco in his own 747. He arrived in a taxi shortly before an unhappy bodyguard drove up in a Jaguar. The bodyguard had been expected to meet the 747. When Ken Snyder, the priest saw Gordon's name on the register as a witness he said "You have the same name as that millionaire". Gordon replied "I am that millionaire". I sympathized with Gordon.

Even at the wedding of his friend he was beset by people looking for grants. One of the advantages of not being a millionaire is the knowledge that people who say they like you are not interested in your money. They just like you. At the reception which followed the wedding. Betty and I were surrounded by family and friends. It was a joyous occasion.

The Lewis/Burke wedding party

Susan Pietsch and Scott Haas rented the hall for their wedding/reception. I was standing in the lobby when a car pulled up to the entrance and a man yelled "Where I bring peeg?" He had a whole pig on a spit which was later paraded into the hall. Following the wedding, lavish tables of food were laid out beneath the advertising screen. During the reception the same man kept beating on a pot saying "Come, why you not eat peeg?" The answer was simple. The family of the bride and their friends were all vegetarians. Twelve members of the Radost Balkan Dancing Troupe ensured wild dancing during the reception. Three musicians played. The player of the large bass violin got too enthusiastic and drove the peg of his instrument into its wooden body. Another group had left a bass violin for us to store. Betty told the bass player he could use it only if he were more restrained.

Mike Conkle's wedding to Karen Mataya was a real production. During the ceremony, Karen turned to him and belted out "You are so beautiful" to augment her "I do". While photos were being taken in the lobby and in Kobe Park, the guests rearranged the hall to have tables set for the reception.

Mike Conkle and Karen Mataya Wedding   130A

Karen Mataya   130B

The wedding of Alexandra Corddry and Norman Porter Langill was another musical event. The friends attending were each handed an "Audio-nuptial participatory device (kazoo)" which they used to play the wedding march.

The theatre venue itself set the theme for the wedding of Karyn Mori and Randy Paris. Tickets labeled "One Performance Only" were required for those attending the event. A theatre program was issued at the door. Rev. Shinseki of White River Buddhist Temple officiated.

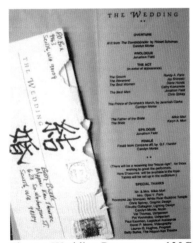
Theatre Wedding Program   130C

Religious Groups

In addition to the many weddings which took place in the Nippon Kan, the hall had other religious uses.

The first year of operation saw a performance of "Heaven can Wait" produced by the Japanese Presbyterian Church School. The church returned for *Faith Like a Child* and *The Ichthus Syndrome* both produced by Joyce Bhang. In 1984 the Japanese Baptist Church produced the musical *Christian Games*. The Cherry Hill Baptist Church sponsored *The Old Ship of Zion* by Wil/Har Productions.

In 1986 the Everyday Christian Ministries (EDCM) used the hall for the first time. The leaders of the congregation were Patti and Julius Young. They believed that churches, their construction and maintenance, detracted from an emphasis on Christian virtues. The group became a regular user of the Nippon Kan for their services. The group did not celebrate holy days because members believed each day was holy. Their services were joyful and many in the congregation spoke in tongues. They reached out and helped those in need. The group used the hall once a week until we left the theatre.

Fund Raisers

The Nippon Kan became an important site for political fund raisers because it was neutral ground. Rather than go to separate Asian American venues, aspiring office holders could have events at which all of the diverse Asian American communities could be invited and be met. County Council member Ruby Chow was the first to hold an event. Councilmen Bruce Hilyer, Tom Weeks and Jim Street, Councilwomen Jane Noland and Janice Niemi, Mayor Charles Royer, Senator Mike Lowry, Congressman McDermott, Governor Gardner and Governor Gary Locke, all had campaign fund raisers in the Nippon Kan. Vice Presidential candidate Geraldine Ferrero's campaign committee placed a large sign on the building and this upset the financial investor in the building. He had to concede that she had a right to advertise her own event in the theatre. We were out of town on the night of the fund raiser and missed the excitement when our Vietnamese janitor bumped into secret servicemen on the backstairs leading to the theatre.

The Wing Luke Museum held its annual auction in the hall during the years we were managing the Nippon Kan. We would bid on items and ultimately had quite a few possessions we would otherwise not have acquired and did not need.

At a Mountaineer's auction I bid on a guided climb of Mt. Hood for two. The guides were two very experienced climbers, one of them a State Supreme Court Judge. Betty didn't want to go so I took my eldest daughter Linda on the trip. Linda didn't like the climb but once she reached to top she was hooked. She later became an avid climber and married Kevin Broderick, AIA, a fellow enthusiast.

Author and daughter Linda   132

Neighborhood House

This organization provided social services and activities for residents of the Seattle Housing Association. Karen Ko arranged for them to have a Halloween party in 1985 and from that point on they returned each year sometimes twice a year.

Discos

Given our good experience the first year with the Asian Student Association of UW Betty decided that we would continue use of the hall for dances but with certain provisos. The discos were noisy and we were located close to senior housing. Betty insisted that noise levels at dances be kept below the point where she could hear them on the opposite side of the street from the theatre. She also insisted that a security guard be present in the hall during dances for the protection of the hall and the young people in attendance. In addition, for High School events, parent chaperones were required. We were also in attendance for all but the last disco held in the Nippon Kan. Sixty disco dances were held in the hall between 1981 and

1990. With few exceptions the young people respected the Nippon Kan and treated it well.

The Rainier Beach High School Prom was an early dance that absolutely bombed. The band members were older than those attending. Their music was outdated by the standards of the young people who hired them and the sound level was far too high. Most of the students stayed crowded in the lobby or stood outside the entrance. The same students returned two weeks later for a happier event, dancing to the music provided by disc jockey Ed Locke.

Disco promotion shirt   133A

Dance Poster   133B

We had some unusual groups hold dances. The Dyketones, a single gender group, rented the hall. I was upstairs in my office but came down to see if Betty needed help. Several girls had removed their upper garments and were dancing with great enthusiasm. Betty sent me back upstairs. The discos provided an opportunity for young Asian Americans to meet and socialize. One of the Japanese American students involved in our first disco organized the annual New Year's Eve disco catering to young Asian Americans. We stopped leasing the hall to him one year before we left the theatre. The character of the young people attending had changed. They had no regard for the history of the Nippon Kan. We had left the young man who arranged the dances in charge while we attended a concert at Saint James Cathedral. We returned to discover that an altercation had taken place and that there was a possibility that those ousted from the hall might return with weapons. This did not occur but we called the police as a precaution. We decided that the era of dances in the hall was over.

Difficult Events

To coin a phrase, "The price of a well maintained hall is eternal vigilance." We were required to intervene to protect the hall on several occasions.

The Vietnamese reception was one of these. Betty found one of the food servers squatting on the floor of the hall and chopping pork using our oak floor as a cutting board. Amazingly, the organizer later requested another use of the hall.

At one event an elderly Issei lit up a cigarette in spite of signs in Japanese prohibiting smoking. I explained the hazard to the hall in English but finally had to use my limited Japanese to say smoking is bad. He was not happy with the message or my Japanese.

A Wiccan group held a dance. Betty had nothing against the group's beliefs but when they damaged the toilets they were told not to come back.

At a Bahai event two young boys decided to clog the toilets with toilet paper. A plumber was called to unclog the toilets. In the interim, one of the adults shuttled his friends to the toilets in his office four blocks away so the event could continue. It was at this point that I found that the renovation contractor had placed the drains at the high point of the toilet rooms.

One college fraternity was required to shut its dance down early. They had thrown objects from the balcony and were caught stealing chairs. Yet another university group showed up totally inebriated. They were told to go home. The benefits of higher education were not evident.

These bad events were few and far between. Maintenance of the hall was kept at a high level and our example helped. If we saw something dropped on the floor we picked it up. I still am compelled to pick up papers dropped on the floor when I attend a theatre. I also find myself hovering near the hall entrances as if to greet people or wish them goodnight.

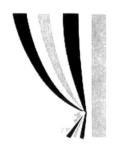

Chapter 12
The Grand Finale

Heartsong Institute

Marlene Anderson brought Heartsong to the Nippon Kan several times. Heartsong was a group of singers who truly enjoyed performing together. Their early performances were to raise funds to visit Russia. They did not always have pre arranged venues in Russia in which to perform but traveled, made friends and found welcoming people. When they didn't have a place to play in Moscow they just set up on a corner of Red Square and sang anyway. After they returned to Seattle the Goodwill Games took place and Heartsong took advantage of the cultural exchange program. They ran a show for seventeen nights in the hall. Several of the small groups they had met in Russia came to Seattle and wanted to say they had performed in the U.S. Marlene asked if the Russian performers could follow the Heartsong concerts as a form of encore. We agreed. Each night a different Russian ensemble would play. They had transportation from Russia but had no money for other expenses so they relied on donations from the audience. We enjoyed the music immensely. Unfortunately, each ensemble elected to play "Kalinka" as one of their songs. At the end of the series we had Kalinka in our heads for weeks. This final week was one of late nights but great fellowship.

Poster   135

End of an Era

In 1991 Betty and I left the theatre. Betty had built up the use of the Nippon Kan to the point it had reached before the Evacuation. Thirty events were scheduled in our last month. The Kobe Park Building office space was fully occupied. So why did we leave?

Operating the hall took hard work. Betty had long hours starting at 9:00 in the morning and sometimes ending at 2:00 the following morning. The theatre was physically demanding. I maintained an architectural practice and then at the end of the day joined Betty to help with events by arranging tables and chairs and setting stage lights. When hall users did not clean up properly Betty and I completed the work. But these operational aspects were not significant in our decision to leave the hall. Disagreement with our partner drove us to leave.

The partnership had been beset with problems from the outset. In order to meet cost overruns and comply with our partnership agreement we borrowed heavily from family and friends. Paying these obligations impacted our lives and my architectural practice. Our major tenant reneged on its lease after one year. Our partner had a guaranteed return on his investment well in excess of the project's income. We received no return on our investment. Our agreement gave our partner all of the tax benefits of the project. Each year of operation our equity in the project was reduced and that of our partner increased. This eventually gave him majority ownership and control of the Kobe Park Building. Our partner demanded an increase in the rent we paid for our space in excess of the rents of comparable space in a brand new adjacent building. I tried but was unable to dissolve the partnership.

Management of the Nippon Kan was the point on which we had our major disagreement. The partner asked that I seek bids to replace Betty as lessee of the Nippon Kan. Without Betty's hands on management I knew that the life of the Nippon Kan would be extinguished. As a matter of principle we took our losses and walked away. Our judgment unfortunately proved correct. Without Betty's presence the hall deteriorated rapidly and was recently converted into the dispatch room for a legal messenger service company.

Postlude

While we regretted the loss of the Nippon Kan we appreciated the wonderful times we had enjoyed and all the friends we had made. We had the opportunity to serve as temporary custodians of an important part of Seattle History. We contributed to the advancement of new music and awareness of Japanese culture in Seattle and gave pleasure to untold numbers of hall users.

While the Nippon Kan no longer exists as a performance venue, we made sure that its role in Seattle history would not be forgotten. All of our historic materials, programs, photos and hand written records are now on file at the University of Washington. All of our photo slides and music cassettes were donated to the Wing Luke Asian Museum. The untold history has been recorded. This narrative should fill in the gaps.

Shortly after we left the project we purchased a small motor home, gave our worldly goods to our children and took to the road. I paint watercolors which can be seen at WWW.edburkewatercolors.com . Betty kept a journal of our travels. We traveled around the United States and across Canada twice and drove through every state of Mexico.

In 2007 when Betty was diagnosed with stage four cancer she declined chemotherapy and chose to die in Ajijic, a Mexican village we both enjoyed. She was surrounded with friends, sunshine and the birds she loved. She had accomplished much in her life and died peacefully December 25th. 2010. This book is a tribute to her memory.

Appendices

Seattle Symphony Orchestra New Music Series

1985 **September 18th** Schwarz conducted Stephen Albert's *Treestone* and *River Run;* Charles Griffes   *Three Tone Pictures;* Roger Bouland's *Seven Pollock Paintings* and George Perle's *Serenade no.3 for Piano and Chamber Orchestra.* Albert, Perle and Bourland were present.

1986 **January 17th** Schwarz conducted works by Varese, Druckman, Tower and Panufnik.
May 28th Schwarz conducted; Karen Hall, soprano sang in a piece by Riegger. Music by Thorne, Swilich and Schoenberg was also played.
September 17th Perry Sperry, tenor was featured and works by Rochberg, Rouse, Maderna, Dallapeccola and Rand were played.
November 10th Schwarz conducted works by Kolb, Bergsma, Schwanter, Babbit and Crumb and in addition played *Sheet of Music* by Kolb.

1987 **February 12th** Schwarz conducted Carol Weber, soprano and Walter Grey, cellist in works by Villa-Lobos, Chavez, Schnitke, Herbolsheimer (Seattle composer) and Albert.
September 16th *Compositions from Britain* included works by Bennet, Bedford, Birdwistle, Lipkin and Bainbridg.
November 8th as part of **Performa 87** Schwarz conducted: Andrzej Panufnik, *Autumn Music;* Webern, *Concerto Opus 24;* Perle, *Lyric Intermezzo (World Premiere);* Beaset, *Songs from the Occasions;* and Tsontakis, *The Past, The Passion.*

1988 **May 11th** Christopher Kendall conducted works by Wernick, Perera, Foss and Danielpour with Carmen Pelton, soprano.
September 16th Schwarz conducted Louise Marley, mezzo with Bogdashevskaya, piano in works by Panufnik, Druckman, Harbison and Messiaen.

1989 **February 24th** Kendall conducted Madeline Rivera, soprano in works by Tower. Schoenberg and Maw.
May 19th Schwarz conducted Thomasa Eckert, soprano, Duane Hulbert, piano in works by Diane Thome, Schwanter, Albert and John Gibson

Marzena Events

1986 **June 3rd Performance of** music by Kodo Araki II & V, Takemitsu, Berio, Henze and Schwanter. Performers included Stuart Dempster, trombone, Thomasa Eckert, soprano, Don McKenzie,   guitar, Tom Moran, mandolin, Trudy Sussman, flutes, Pamela Vokolek, harp and Kathleen Hunter, dancer.
November 4th Works by Bergsma, Priest, Schwanter, Corigliano and Lennon were performed. Tom Stiles was stage manager, Rose Lee provided a floral display and Leslie Fried designed the   set,

1987 **March 5th** Music by Zimmerman, Kuss/Glen, Sciarrino, Kurtag, Meyer, Wapp, Priest, Strauss and Somers.
May 8th Markus Stockhausen, trumpet performed his father Karlheinz Stockhausen's work.
May 27th Works by Thome, Messiaen, Harvey, Dutilleux, Priest, Jones, Harley and Sugai.
December 9th & 11th Vesali Icones and other works from Britain, Canada and the U.S. A powerful dance interpretation of Christ's Passion; the crushing strength of industrialization in a tone poem for piano and a moving dramatic piece about a vicious Scottish teacher. Performers included Kabby Mitchell, dancer, Alexander Segal, cello and five others conducted by Karen Thomas. Jean Sherrard, actor.

1988 **April 7th and 8th** *First Annual Seattle Spring.* Composers Yun, Xenakis, Priest, Strauss and Stone. Wade Madsen, actor, Jo Feffingwell, actress.
June 16th & 17th *Ursula K LeGuin* Poetry and music. Works by Ligeti, Schlee & Schwantner.

1989 **January 19th & 20th** *Bulgarian and Romanian Music* Alexander Illitch Eppler on Kaval and Cimbalom, Joan Purswell, piano, Alexander Segal, cello, Eric Shumski, viola. Works by Messiaen, Scelsi, Priest, Durko, Ginastera and Kurtag.
April 12th *Second Annual Seattle Spring Festival of Contemporary Music* Opening night preview party, Fred Hauptman, moderator.
April 14th *Music, Dance & Drama World Premieres* by Kathleen Hunt, Scott Lakin Jones, Thomas Peterson, Jean Sherrard and John Zoltak. In addition works by Franco Donatoni, Jonathan Harvey, Ennio Morricone and Robert Rosen were performed.
April 20th *Criminal Acts* featured Seth Krimsky, bassoon; EWI & Attitude. *Other works by strange people with foreign names* aided and abetted by Sandra Bleiweiss and Mathew Kocmieroski. The theme of the program was "Expect the Unexpected".
April 21st Alexander Segal, cello, assisted by Dianne Chilgren playing works by Jon Deak, Henri Dutilleux, Alberto Ginastera, Witold Lutoslawski, Krzysztof Meyer, Penderecki and Isang Yun.
October 26th *Octoberfest* Music and Dance works by Daniel Asia, Stuart Dempster, John Anthony Lennon, Wade Massen and Joan Franks Williams. Psych-Acoustics and Strip Poker.
October 27th *Music and Theatre Works* by George Benjamin, Jesse Bernstein, Heinz Hollinger, Seth Krimsky, Pet Leinonen, Tristan Murail, Robert Priest and Jean Sherrard.
October 29th *Composer Portrait Works* by Isang Yun

1990	**April 8th** *The Third Annual Seattle Spring* the Festival Preview Party brought a panel discussion "Yes but is it music?" Panelists included Beaver Chief, spiritual drummer, Emilie Berendson, mezzo, Ed Birdwell, Managing Director Seattle Symphony, Jeff Domoto, trombonist in the Emerald City Brass Quintet, Matt Kocmieroski, percussionist director of New Performance Group, Mark Kuss, composer President Washington Composers Forum, Robert Priest, Composer, artistic director Marzena, Trimpin, composer and instrument builder. The moderator was Fred Hauptman, Seattle Weekly Music Critic.

April 13th *Susan Botti*, soprano/composer performs works by Botti, Berio, Wes York, Tan Dun and Gyorgy Kurtag.

April 14th *The International Front* Works by Patrich Marcland, Paul Mefano, Renaud Francois, Giacinto Scelsi, Iannis Xenakis, Berio, Adam-Walrand, William O. Smith, Isan Yun, Simon Bainbridge, Performers included Franck Avril, oboe, Kim Fay, clarinet, Kathleen Hunt, dancer, Joan Purswell, piano, Rovin Clavreul, cello, Motter Forman, harp, Lise Mann, flute and Eric Shumsky, viola.

April 20th *Days of Wind and Moon* Works by Jahnny Reinhard,Thomas Daniel Schlee, Giacinto Scelsi, Bernstein/Beaver Chief/Hunt, Seth Krimsky/Johnny Reinhard, Panufnik, Robert Priest and Jay Mabin performed by Beaver Chief, drummer, Stephen J. Bernstein, actor, Kathleen Hunt, dancer, Seth Krimsky, bassoon, Jay Mabin, harmonica, Don McKenzie, guitar, Joan Purswell, piano and Johhy Reinhard, bassoon.

April 21st *All Russian Program* Works by Shostakovich, Edison Denisov, Gubaidulina, Schnittke, Alexander Illitch Eppler (balalaika) and Paul Taub.

April 25th *Music in the Environment* Works by R Murray Schafer; Documentary films presented by Schafer.

April 26th *Sound and Theatre* Music by R. Murray Schafer; Music for the Morning of the World; Le Cri de Merlin; Wizard Oil and Indian Sagwa.

April 27th Music by R. Murray Schafer performed by the Purcell Strings Quartet.

April 28th Music by R. Murray Schafer performed by the Purcell Strings. Schafer, Emilie Berendsen and Naomi Kato present.

Washington Composers Forum Events (later NW Composers Alliance)

1986	**January 6th** The first concert included Karen Thomas' *Cowboy Songs* followed by Bern Herbolsheimer's *Phoenix Variations,* performed by Bellarmy, Eckart, Nelson, Mann and Phillips. Karen and Bern both had several pieces played in the hall under the aegis of Composers Forum.

1986	**September 27th** works by Kosch, Carl, Lieberman, David Kechley and Bestor were performed. Karen Thomas conducted Lise Mann, flute, MacCantrell, clarinet, Meg Brennand, cello, Mathew Kocmieroski, percussion, Roger Nelson, piano, Thomasa Eckert, soprano, Margaret Berry, horn, Christene Olasen, violin, Mark Hoover, piano, Kimm Brocket, alto sax, Bev Setzer, bass clarinet, Sarah Weiner, oboe and English horn.

December 10th an evening of electronic music.

1987	**May 28th** Music for Brass performed by the Emerald City Brass Quintet. Works by Ebert, Monroe, Reid, Shoemaker, Mountain, Thomas and Weston.

1988	**February 15th** *Sound Now Series* composers Scott Lakin Jones, Karen
P, Thomas, Clement Reid, Alan Fuellheim, Gregory Yasinitsky and Kendall Durelle Briggs.

March 9th *Sound Now Series* composers Gabel, Buchman, Belden, Scott Jones and Knapp.

April 9th Composers Kuss, Karen Thomas, Underhill, Reid and Yasinitsky.

May 15th Multi-media works. Dripphony for viola & original instruments featuring the Aquaphone, created by Barbara Bernstein, Jerry Mayer and Bill Linen. Dancers performed in Automobile composed by Jackie Gabel.

November 20th Works by Bergsma, Sugai, Kuss & Patterson.

1989	**February 28th** Works by Sam-Ang Sam, Argersinger, Buchman, Kuss, Scott Lakin Jones and Buell.

March 16th Camas (formerly NW Wind Quintet) performed works by Jones, Ysinitsky, Heins & Bergsma.

April 15th *Sound Now Series Concert #4.* Puget Sound Flute Quartet playing works by Mathew Hasser Bennett, Paul Eliott, David Jones and Scott Lakin Jones. **In Memorium** Thomas Peterson and Ciro Scotto.

April 17th *Music of Josef Vodak.*

April 23rd *Festival of Piano Works by NW Composers* Joel Salsman, piano, Leon Lishner, bass and John Zielinski perormed works by Bergsma, Leonard Berkowitz, Alan Hovhaness, Eero Richmond, Carol Sams, Diane Thome and John Verrall.

May 14th Pam Dolan, soprano, John Sielinski, piano, Gregory Short, piano, NWCA Chamber Players and Joel Salsman, piano played works by Dvorak, Gregory Short, Hovhaness, Andre Tchaikovsky and John Verrall.

1990	**January 27th** *Sound Now Series* Works by Hovhaness, Clement Reid, Carol Shoemaker & David Hunter.

February 26th *Sound Now Series* The Vancouver Pro-Musica-Soundscape 1990. Works by Armanini, Patric Caird and Dennis Burke.

April 16th *Sound Now Series* Works by Joan Franks Williams, Mark Kuss, Ciro Scotto, Wrick Wolff and John Zoltek performed by Susan Kohler, clarinet, Jeff Domoto, trombone, Phyllis Allport, cello, Roger Nelson, piano, Paul Taub, flute, Pamela Ryker, flute, David Gorgas, guitar, Mishelle Curtis, violin, Leslie Johnson, viola and Virginia Dziekonski, cello.

Soundworks Programs

1984 **December 8th** *Anthony Davis*, piano.

1985 **September 14th** *Music for the Harmonic Piano,* Michael Harrison.
   October 12th Music of David Mahler, Stuart Dempster & Eric Jensen.
   October 20th *Songs of One, Two, Three, Four or more Note* by Alvin Curran.
   November 30th *New Music for Bowed Piano* by Stephen Scott.
   December 6th Music of Ingram Marshal.

1986 **June 20th & 21st** Jay Hamilton's concert performance of opera "Ippi" with Quixote String Ensemble.
   June 26th Ron Blake, piano playing work by Herb Levy.
   November 1st Rova Saxophone Quartet.
   November 15th Gamela Pacifica
   November 22nd *Electro-Acoustic Music.* Work by Rene Fabre.
   December 13th *ROOM Live Electronic Music*

1987 **November 8th** *Performa 87* Music of Jay Hamilton *Zahhak,* Steve Layton *Creaming Songs* , David Mahler *Cadent Remarks,* Thomas Peterson *Night Images* and Karen Thomas *The Lone Ranger* performed by *The New Performance Group* with Thomasa Eckert duded up and Walter Gray in a cowboy outfit strumming his cello on his lap and singing. Diane Schenker was the narrator.
   March 10th *Earshot Jazz* The Robert Holcomb Band and The Horvitz Morris Previte Trio.
   June 23rd *Earshot Jazz* Tony Williams Quintet
   June 28th *Earshot Jazz* Bill Frisell Quartet
   June 29th *Earshot Jazz* Carla Bley/Steve Swallow Trio
   July 1st *Earshot Jazz* Craig Harris and Tailgater's Tales.
   November 7th *Earshot Jazz* The Oliver Lake Quartet
   November 21st *Earshot Jazz* Robin Holcomb
   November 28th *Earshot Jazz* Alan Youngblood Quintet with Hadley Caliman and Julian Priester.
   December 13th *Earshot Jazz* Blood Ulmer with Jamaaladeen Tacuma and Calvin Weston, one hand clapping.

In 1990 Soundworks took advantage of the **Goodwill Games** funding to put on an *International Computer Music Festival.* Events took place on July 5th, 6th, 7th 12th 13th 14th 15th and 17th. The works of nineteen composers were played.

Recital Performers and Chamber Groups

1981 Jim W. Johnson Piano Recital
   William Primrose gala Concert
   Jazz at the Nippon Kan I, Robert Antolin
   Aolian Ensemble Richard Weeks, oboe
   Piano and Voice at the Nippon Kan Sheila Siobhan Burke, soprano, Nancy Louise Cobbs, piano;
   Jazz at the Nippon Kan II International District Band
   Washington Jazz Society Woody Woodhouse

1982 *Chamber Music* Frank Kowalski, clarinet; Jacqueline Hofto, flutist, Katherine Collier, pianist and Vizhak Schotten, violist.
   Voice Recital, Sheila Siobhan Burke, soprano, Glenda Williams, piano
   Twentieth Century Piano Works Keva L. Vaughan, piano;
   In Concert Ira Jones;
   Piano Recital, Jim W. Johnson
   Evergreen Opera Theatre Stephen Humphrey, director, Joseph Crnko, musical director, Julie Mirel, Charles Wayne, Stephen Tachell, Gary Jordan, Linda Cusanelli, Peter Ashbaugh and Frank Guarrera, singers;
   Piano Recital Espee Endrata, Flora Dacanay;

1983 *Keva Vaughan, Pianist*
   An Evening of Song Sheila Siobhan Burke, soprano, Glenda Williams, piano;
   To Suzanne with Love Singers gala with Peter Ashbaugh, Shirley Harned, Mira Frohnmeieer, Victoria Millor, Marian Weltmann, Kelly McPherson, Gus Paglialunga and Monserrat Alavedra;
   Five Poems by Andre Breton by Esther Sugai, singer, instruments, tape and dancer;
   Guitar Pedro Bacan;

1984 *Concert for Peace Nuclear Exchange* Keva Vaughan, piano, Gretchen Hewitt, Toby Saks;
   Seattle Pro Musica Joyce Gibbs, piano;
   Philadelphia String Quartet;
   Peter Ashbaugh Farewell Linda Cusinelli, Jackie Schneider, Norman Smith, Shirley Harned and Sheila Burke;

Winterreise, Franz Schubert Beat Hadorn, bass, George Fiore, piano;
Santa Fe Chamber Music Festival I Kenneth Cooper, harpsichord, Deborah Carley Emory, Harris   Goldsmith;
Santa Fe Musical Festival II Leslie Howard, piano, Alan Titus, baritone, Alicia Schachter, accompanist.
Chamber Music Washington Troubadours, Keva Vaughn, piano, Betty Agent, viola, Deborah Yamak, cello and Gretchen Hewitt, voice;
Artists in America Celeste and Chris Trembanis, vocalists, Stan Purvis, clarinet, Dan Shelhamer, piano,
Recital Deborah Yamak, cello, Laurel Anderson, piano;
Larry Cross Voice Recital
Tosca in Concert produced by Seattle POPS Opera, Dan Shelhamer, Director;

1985   *Chamber Music* Page Smith, cello, Marjorie Kransberg-Talvi, violin, Keven Aanerud, piano;
Chamber Music Penelope Crane, viola, Lisa Bergman, piano, Zartouhi Dombourian-Eby, flute, Roberta Hansen Downey, cello;
Violin Recital Students of Margaret Pressley;
Piano Recital Larry Cross students;
For the Love of Singing and the Singing of Love Marlene Anderson, soprano,   Jack Mabbott, tenor, Jerry Zimmerman, piano, Steve Klein, bass, Christopher Caldwell, Director;
Duo Flautists Pamela Mooney and Karla Flygare, Lisa Bergman, piano;
Betty Martin Williams, Saphire Productions

1986   *The Sonora Quartet* Fred Halgedahl, violin, Ella Marie Gray, violin, Catherine Brubaker, viola and Walter Gray, cello;
Benefit Recital Seattle University, Music for Two Pianos Patricia Bowman and Cassandra Carr.
Sound of Seattle Music Fest Stephen Banks and the Seatown Orchestra, Romance Hilliard, Raw Silk and the Deems 7 Group;
Recital Jennie Clegg, soprano, Chris Trembanis, baritone, Beth Kirschoff, piano;
Puget Sound Flute Quartet Pamela Ryker;
Recital Terry Cook, cello, Tony Padilla, piano;
Hollywood Underground Cabaret;
Uncommon Partners Music Series Kay Gardener, flute, composer and healer with Linda   Waterfall, acoustic artist;
Sounds of the Soaring Heart Al Harris, Bill Mann and Ilona Sundstrup-Harris;
Foundation for the Caressa Strad Kristi Bjarnason and Victor Steinhardt;
Piano Recital Jane Harty (related to composer Hamilton Harty) premiered Night Fantasies by Elliot Carter;
Recital Students of Charles Bommarito.
Anything Goes Jacalyn Schneider, soprano, Joan Blyth, piano;
Penelope Crane, Lisa Bergman, Ella Gray Recital
Seattle Young Artists Sixteenth Annual Music Festival
Benefit Recital Katheryne Bishop, soprano, Terry Spiller, piano;
Vocal Recital Brian Bernado
The Saxaphone Quartet;
Chileans for Democracy Charles Murphy's Band

1987   *Silverwood* Trudy Sussman Antolin, flute, Naomi Kato, harp, Penelope Crane, viola, Ella Marie Gray, violin, Thomasa Eckert, voice;
Seattle University Faculty Recital Series Arthur Barnes, piano.
Early Forte piano & Clavichord Joan Benson;
Piano Recital Alisa Moshinsky's adult students;
Seattle University Faculty Artist Recital Jacalyn Schneider, soprano, Joan Blyth, piano;
Visionary Experience in Music Piano Concert David Messmer, composer;
Seattle University Faculty Recital Series Joan Martin Woodard, viola, Walter Gray, cello, Lise Mann, flute, Cassandra Carr, piano, Arthur Barnes, piano;
Music for Marimba by Japanese Composers Mathew Kocmieroski;
Music of the German Baroque Janet See, flute, Sandra Scharz, violin, Margriet Tindemans, viola da gamba, Margaret Gries, harpsichord;
Sigma Alpha Iota Laura Hamm, flute, Pae Wen Tsai, piano;
Seattle University Faculty Artist Series Patricia Bowman and Cassandra Carr, piano duettists;
The Bel Canto Quartet Janeanne Houston, soprano, Barton Green, tenor, Marcia Bellamy, mezzo,   Norman Smith, bass;
Recital Kathryn Weld, Steve Tachell, George Shangrow;
Blockhouse Productions Pedar Herom;
An Afternoon's Delight Lisa Sutphen, soprano, Sheila Whalen, piano and the A Capella Quartet;
Recital Theresa Williams, soprano;
The Evening of Twentieth Century Music Terry Cook, cello, Joel Salsman, piano;
Whisper of the Muse Helen McNab, vocalist, Sylvia Taylor, piano;
Peder Herom Live;
Dreams that Fall to Earth Andrew Glen, solo concert dance & mime;
Bela Siki Piano Concert

1988   *Northwoods Wind Quintet & Magic Circle Mime Co.* Roupen Shakarian, composer, "FOOLS" set   to a story by Douglas MacIntyre "Fear and Loathing of Classical Music, Part 1" for actors & musicians. Eric Stokes, Phonic Paradigm #1, Berio, Opus Number Zoo, David Jones, Woodwind Quintet No 1;
Nancy Zylstra, Soprano, Bern Herbolsheimer, Piano Music by Rossini, Strauss, Herbolsheimer and others.
Intimate Friends, a Musical Celebration Rising Phoenix, Miriam Moses, Ruth Barton, lights;
A Songfest for Valentine's Day Sheila Siobhan, soprano, William Lewis, tenor, Bern Herbolsheimer, piano;
Concert Nancy Zylstra, soprano, Janet See, baroque flute, Margriet Tindemans, viola da gamba, Jillon Stoppels Dupree, harpsichord;

Songs of the Danube Rainier Chorale;
Works by NW Composers McKay, Verral, Bergsma, Thome, Hovhaness, Kechley and Beale Joel Salsman, piano;
Kicking the Clouds Away Vocalmotion cabaret;
Big Band Concert Seattle Jazz Orchestra, Jazz Police;
David Ritt in Recital Works for trombone;
Terry Anderson Kallenberg, Flute, Lisa Bergman, Piano
Pedar Herom & Charlie Kopp
Trumpet Recital, Richard Pressley;
The Ferryboat Musicians Kat & Steve Guth;
An Afternoon of Passionate Music Terry Palasz, soprano;
Gerry Garcia Seattle Music Company;
Henry Eugene Hart Voice Recital;
Earthwings in Concert Eddie Zuniga, dancer choreographer
Terry Cook, Cello, Kevin Byford, guitar, Joyce Gibb, piano;
Swan Productions Presents "In Concert" Gretchen Hewitt, soprano, Keva McMorrow, pianist;
Northwoods Wind Quintet Magic Circle Mime Co Clown musician;
Santa Fe Music Festival Artist's Circle Recital Carter Brey, cello, Christopher O'Riley, piano;

1989 *Pedor's Performances* Kym Tuvim, singer/song writer, Robert Lester's vibes, Myra Goldfarb's passionate dance debut;
Roosevelt High School Jazz Band Band Boosters, Chuck Chinn V.P.;
Friends for Life Concert NW Aids Foundation;
Evening of Classical Keyboard Music Jerome Pauson;
Suzuki Spring Concert
Masters Graduation Recital Sang Hee Lee, harp;
An Evening With St Kahn Folk Songwriter Performance Western States Center;
Opera and Operetta Michael McCall, tenor, Ralph Wells, baritone, Michael Barnes, piano (performed first scene from "Plump Jack" by Gordon Getty);
Charlie Kopp & Jim Lyon Trio;
Cambiata Chamber Music Concert Allegro Wind Quartet Sue Steil, flute, Gwen Lewis, cello, Rebecca Clemens, violin, Yollanda Ionescu,   piano;
Christopher Caldwell, Yours for a Song, a Musical Entertainment Diane Zebert, director;
Centrum Summer Sampler in Seattle Flying Karamazov Brothers, The Bud Shank Jazz Quartet, Fiddle Tunes All Stars, Flamenco Fiesta, Jim Whittaker & the Mount Everest Peace Climb Team, Peggy Platt;
Theresa Williams, Soprano, Beth Kirchhoff, piano;
Meryl Ettelson, Pianist;
Dancewax Musical Comedy Ray Kaltenbach, Camille Chrysler, choreographer;
Jeffrey Francis, Tenor, Bern Herbolsheimer, Piano;
Piano Recital Phyllis Lee students;
Recital Ann Cummings, piano;
Carolyne Maia, mezzo, Johanna Mastenbrook, Piano, Paul Taub, Flute, Craig Weaver, Cello & The Salieri String Quartet presented by Music Room;
Recital Jan Ekstedt, violin, Kanen Janes, Piano;
Sol Ancantara, Baritone, Dante Cabasco, Pianist;

1990 *Graz Scholarship Gala* Sheila Siobhan, soprano, Sara Hedgepeth, mezzo, Christine Peters, soprano;
Nacht und Traume, A Song Recital Randel Wagner & Laura Ward;
New Music for Solo Guitar Patrick Berry, composer & guitarist.
Recital Lorrie D. Northey, piano
Works for Unaccompanied Cello Eugene Zenzen
Emerald City Brass Quintet Works by Lutoslawski, John Metcalf, Claude Baker, John Harbison, Phillip Lambro, Karen P. Thomas, Jan Bach. Performers, William Berry, David Hensler, Margaret Berry, Jeff Domoto and Robert Searle;
Vocal Motion Farewell Celebration Lark Young;
New Works for Saxophone Modal Music Productions;
Sax Billy Tipton Memorial Saxophone Quartet, Vinny Golia Group;
Sax One Hand Clapping, Joseph Jarman-Thurman Baker Duo;
Schweiger Suzuki Spring Recital;
Spring Recital Piano students of Jennifer Hammill;
Recital Students of Satomi Pellerin;
Amharic Ethiopian Performance
An Evening of Inspiration and Music Alia Barbera Mastro & Terry Cole Whitaker;
Piano Recital Liping Sun;
First Slavic Full Gospel Choir of Ballard;
Five Great Sonatas Janene Shigley, flute, John Zielinski, piano.

Weddings and Wedding Receptions

1981   Ann Cole and John Peugh
Debbie Uno and Danny Uno

1982   Karen Mataya and Mike Conklin
Laurie Keefe and Robert Le May
Heidi Bodding and Ronald Long

1983   Gayle Miyahara and Brad Miyaki
Janet Kamada and Brian Masuo

1984   Jennifer Beaton and Lyle Lafond
Sarah Yamasaki and Tom Ikeda

1985   Joyleen Ko and Richard Anzai
Teresa Fukuhara and Jay Mori
Jacqueline McCray and Edward Jackson
Colleen Tressel and Michael Eslinger

1986   Michele Anderson and Danny Finkley
Ann Hidaka

1987   Sherry Claar and Stephen Dennis
Sheila Siobhan Burke and William Lewis
Tom Do
Rita (Elway) Brogan and Michael Richards
Audrey Prewitt and Leroy Taylor
Linda Akemi Hara and Christopher Emile Nelson
Jane Alexandra Corddry and Norman Porter Langill
Teresa Baraguit
Dolores Nakamura

1988   Jeanette Rooks and Dave
David and Misty Niehl Shelton
Marilyn Perry
Kathleen Boe
Karyn Mori and Randy Paris
Sylvia Kirihard and Locke
Patricia Ikeda
Susan Mosborg

1989   Kathryn and Thomas Hunsaker
Lenore Hayes and Gary Bruce Scott
Karen Conley and Ron Webb
Dave Pellerin and Satomi
Jill Kathleen-Marie Schumacher and E. Wallace Ridgewell
Julie Hollander and John C. Smith
Claudia Noel McCormack and Richard Lee Smith

1990   Michele Thompson and Larry Ransom
Amy Thomson and Raymond Ken Takeuchi
Arlene Pringle

Images used as Illustrations.

Most images used in this book are taken from materials which I donated either to the University of Washington or to the Wing Luke Asian Museum and are therefore their property and are used only with their permission. Materials donated to the University of Washington can be found in Burke Associates Accession #4474-002 Boxes 1, 2, 3, 4 and 5. More recently we donated our slide collection to the Wing Luke Asian Museum. This latter material is designated the Burke Collection. The images of early Seattle were modified and used in our prior publication "Seattle's Other History". The images of events which took place in the Nippon Kan before the Evacuation were given by sympathetic friends in the Japanese American community with the knowledge that they could be used in future publications. All images of events in the Nippon Kan following and surrounding its restoration were taken with two exceptions by the author.

Illustration		
	9; 10; 11; 12; 13; 14A.B; 15; 16A,B,C; 17;	University of Washington Libraries, Special Collections
	19A,B,C,D,E; 20; 21A,B; 22;	University of Washington Libraries, Special Collections
	23A,B,C;	Wing Luke Asian Museum
	26A,B; 27; 28; 29A,B; 3B; 2A,B; 33A,B; 34A,B;	University of Washington Libraries, Special Collections
	36A,B; 37A,B,C,D; 38A,B; 39A,B; 40A,B; 41;	University of Washington Libraries, Special Collections
	42A,B; 43A,B; 44A,B; 45; 46A,B; 47; 48A,B;	University of Washington Libraries, Special Collections
	49A,B; 50: 51; 53; 54A,B,C; 55;	University of Washington Libraries, Special Collections
	56; 57; 58; 60; 62;	Wing Luke Asian Museum
	63;	University of Washington Libraries, Special Collections
	64A,B; 65; 66;	Wing Luke Asian Museum
	67A,B;	University of Washington Libraries, Special Collections
	68A,B,C; 70; 71A,B; 72A,B; 73A,B,C;	Wing Luke Asian Museum
	74A,B,C; 75A,B;	Wing Luke Asian Museum
	76;	Dean Wong
	78; 79;A,B; 81; 82A,B,C; 83; 84A,B; 85A,B; 86;	Wing Luke Asian Museum
	87: 88; 89; 91A,B; 92	Wing Luke Asian Museum
	93;	Dean Wong
	94; 96A,B,C; 97A,B,C; 98A,B,C,D; 99A,B; 100;	Wing Luke Asian Museum
	101	Dean Wong
	104A,B; 105A,B; 106; 107;108A,B; 109A,B;	Wing Luke Asian Museum
	111;	University of Washington Libraries, Special Collections
	112A,B;	Wing Luke Asian Museum
	113; 115;	University of Washington Libraries, Special Collections
	116; 117; 118A,B,C;	Wing Luke Asian Museum
	119;	University of Washington Libraries, Special Collections
	121A,B,C,D; 122A,B; 123; 124;	Wing Luke Asian Museum
	125A,B;	University of Washington Libraries, Special Collections
	128A,B; 129; 130A, 132;	Wing Luke Asian Museum
	133A,B;	University of Washington Libraries, Special Collections

Stage curtain graphic used at chapter headings were designed by Yutaka Sasaki.
The book cover was designed by author